VICTOR R. FUCHS

NATIONAL BUREAU OF ECONOMIC RESEARCH

JEAN ALEXANDER WILBURN

BARNARD COLLEGE

PRODUCTIVITY DIFFERENCES

WITHIN THE

SERVICE SECTOR

OCCASIONAL PAPER 102

NATIONAL BUREAU OF ECONOMIC RESEARCH

NEW YORK 1967

Distributed by COLUMBIA UNIVERSITY PRESS

NEW YORK AND LONDON

RELATION OF THE DIRECTORS TO THE WORK AND PUBLICATIONS OF THE NATIONAL BUREAU OF ECONOMIC RESEARCH

1. The object of the National Bureau of Economic Research is to ascertain and to present to the public important economic facts and their interpretation in a scientific and impartial manner. The Board of Directors is charged with the responsibility of ensuring that the work of the National Bureau is carried on in strict conformity with this object.

2. To this end the Board of Directors shall appoint one or more Directors of Research.

3. The Director or Directors of Research shall submit to the members of the Board, or to its Executive Committee, for their formal adoption, all specific proposals concerning researches to be instituted.

4. No report shall be published until the Director or Directors of Research shall have submitted to the Board a summary drawing attention to the character of the data and their utilization in the report, the nature and treatment of the problems involved, the main conclusions, and such other information as in their opinion would serve to determine the suitability of the report for publication in accordance with the principles of the National Bureau.

5. A copy of any manuscript proposed for publication shall also be submitted to each member of the Board. For each manuscript to be so submitted a special committee shall be appointed by the President, or at his designation by the Executive Director, consisting of three Directors selected as nearly as may be one from each general division of the Board. The names of the special manuscript committee shall be stated to each Director when the summary and report described in paragraph (4) are sent to him. It shall be the duty of each member of the committee to read the manuscript. If each member of the special committee signifies his approval within thirty days, the manuscript may be published. If each member of the special committee has not signified his approval within thirty days of the transmittal of the report and manuscript, the Director of Research shall then notify each member of the Board, requesting approval or disapproval of publication, and thirty additional days shall be granted for this purpose. The manuscript shall then not be published unless at least a majority of the entire Board and a two-thirds majority of those members of the Board who shall have voted on the proposal within the time fixed for the receipt of votes on the publication proposed shall have approved.

6. No manuscript may be published, though approved by each member of the special committee, until forty-five days have elapsed from the transmittal of the summary and report. The interval is allowed for the receipt of any memorandum of dissent or reservation, together with a brief statement of his reasons, that any member may wish to express; and such memorandum of dissent or reservation shall be published with the manuscript if he so desires. Publication does not, however, imply that each member of the Board has read the manuscript, or that either members of the Board in general, or of the special committee, have passed upon its validity in every detail.

7. A copy of this resolution shall, unless otherwise determined by the Board, be printed in each copy of every National Bureau book.

(Resolution adopted October 25, 1926,
as revised February 6, 1933, and February 24, 1941)

CONTENTS

TABLES

CHARTS

PREFACE

THIS is the third report to appear as a result of the National Bureau's study of productivity in the service industries, undertaken with the financial assistance of the Ford Foundation. The first two, *Productivity Trends in the Goods and Service Sectors, 1929–61: A Preliminary Survey* and *The Growing Importance of the Service Industries,* were focused at a highly aggregative level; the comparisons made were primarily between the goods and service sectors and among major industry groups.

In the present report, an attempt is made to study productivity at a much finer level of industry detail. Such an approach has some clear limitations. It will not be possible to include all the service industries. Moreover, the danger of errors in the data may be greater than when we work with sector aggregates or broad industry groups. Generalizations can be made only with the greatest caution. Nevertheless, we know from preliminary study that substantial differences in rates of growth of productivity exist within the service sector. It may be that an analysis of such differences would provide some insight as to why services as a group tend to improve their output per man less rapidly than do the goods industries. Furthermore, there are a number of important conceptual problems concerning the measurement of output and input in service industries which are likely to be brought out more clearly by a consideration of detailed industries. Finally, the analysis of changes in productivity over time in selected service industries may provide some guidance for the study of intercountry differences in productivity at a given point in time.

The report that follows consists of two independent studies. In the first, differential trends in productivity across seventeen service industries from 1939 to 1963 are examined. The analysis is largely statistical in nature, relying heavily on correlation and regression techniques. Some interesting differences in productivity trends within the service sector are revealed, but no attempt is made to explore any particular industry in depth.

The second study, by Jean Wilburn, does precisely that. It focuses on the disparate performance of two apparently similar industries—barber shops and beauty shops—and subjects these two industries to a highly detailed analysis. This intensive case study not only provides new insights about an unexplored part of the economy but it also increases our understanding of factors of general importance. These include the implications for productivity of technological change, fashion, size of transaction, labor quality, use of part-timers, and disguised unemployment.

One of the results of the studies presented here is to confirm the conclusion reached by economists who have studied manufacturing industries that productivity and growth tend to be positively correlated. Jean Wilburn's paper, in particular, shows the two-sided nature of this relationship, with technological change stimulating growth through decreases in price and improvements in quality, and the growth of demand stimulating productivity through increases in the size of transactions and decreases in idle time. This report also confirms previous findings that changes in wages across industries are not correlated with changes in productivity.

While many of the results presented here tend to support conclusions that have been reached on the basis of studies of manufacturing, other parts of this report serve to point up significant differences between manufacturing and services. It is hoped that this exploration into relatively unknown territory will highlight the importance of developing better data on the service industries and of broadening the scope of investigations of productivity.

The barber and beauty shop industries provide a good illustration of both points. Together they employ almost as many persons as does the basic steel industry, but they receive only a small fraction of the statistical coverage of the latter industry. Furthermore, such frequently discussed questions as the embodiment or disembodiment of technological change prove to be of little consequence in understanding productivity in these industries as compared with questions such as the use of part-timers, changes in the age of the work force, and developments in the competing nonmarket sectors of the economy.

Both authors have numerous acknowledgments that they are happy to make. The Directors' reading committee, Lloyd G. Reynolds, Murray Shields, and Boris Shishkin, made useful suggestions. The first study has benefited from comments by Edward F. Denison and Solomon Fabricant, and thanks are due Irving Leveson for conscientious preparation of the tables and appendixes. A preliminary version of this study was presented at the 9th General Conference of the International Association for Research in Income and Wealth, Lom, Norway, September, 1965.

Jean Wilburn is happy to acknowledge helpful comments from Gary S. Becker, Solomon Fabricant, F. Thomas Juster, Jacob Mincer, and Anna J. Schwartz, and the research assistance of Irving Leveson, Linda Nasif, and Deborah Sarachek.

Both authors are grateful to Charlotte Boschan for the computer program she developed, to International Business Machines Corporation, for its grant of computer time, to James F. McRee for his editorial assistance, to H. Irving Forman who drew the charts, and to Joyce M. Rose for the skill and care she devoted to the secretarial chores.

Certain data used in this paper were derived by the authors from punched cards furnished under a joint project sponsored by the U.S. Bureau of the Census and the Population Council and containing selected 1960 Census information for a 0.1 per cent sample of the population of the United States. Neither the Census Bureau nor the Population Council assumes any responsibility for the validity of any of the figures or interpretations of the figures published herein based on this material.

VICTOR R. FUCHS
Associate Director of Research

I

A STATISTICAL ANALYSIS OF PRODUCTIVITY

IN SELECTED SERVICE INDUSTRIES

IN THE UNITED STATES, 1939–63

Victor R. Fuchs

1

INTRODUCTION

A TENDENCY for employment to grow more rapidly in the service industries than in the rest of the economy is one of the best-documented aspects of economic growth. In the United States, where we have reasonably good information on the industrial distribution of the employed population for at least the last hundred years, this shift to services has occurred almost without interruption and has been more rapid in recent decades than in the period before 1929. Currently, well over half of total employment is accounted for by wholesale and retail trade, finance, insurance, and real estate; professional, personal, business, and repair services; and general government.

Until 1920, the shift of U.S. employment could, in very large measure, be described simply as a movement from agricultural to nonagricultural pursuits. Employment in commodity-producing industries outside of agriculture tended to grow as rapidly as in the services. In the 1920's, however, service industry employment accelerated relative to the rest of the nonagricultural economy. In the 1930's this shift was very pronounced because the impact of the Depression reinforced the secular trend. In the post-World War II period, services have accounted for virtually all of the net absolute growth of employment, as gains in manufacturing and construction have barely been large enough to offset declines in agriculture and mining. Table I-1 shows the levels and shares of employment by major industry group in 1929, 1939, 1948, and 1963.

The growing importance of the service sector, combined with the prominence now given to problems of economic growth, has resulted in a sharp increase in interest in the productivity of the service industries. It is generally believed that productivity in services has not (and

TABLE I-1

Employment in the United States by Major Industry Group, Selected Years, 1929-63

Industry	1929 Employment (thousands)	1929 Percentage of U.S. Total	1939 Employment (thousands)	1939 Percentage of U.S. Total
Agriculture, forestry, and fishing	9,205	19.9	8,273	17.8
Mining	1,017	2.2	870	1.9
Construction	2,306	5.0	1,864	4.0
Manufacturing	10,556	22.8	10,086	21.6
Transportation	3,034	6.6	2,169	4.7
Communications and public utilities	1,034	2.2	871	1.9
Government enterprise	409	.9	503	1.0
Wholesale trade	1,744	3.8	1,942	4.2
Retail trade	6,077	13.1	6,440	13.8
Finance and insurance	1,207	2.6	1,066	2.3
Real estate	368	.8	494	1.1
Households and institutions	3,249	7.0	3,033	6.5
Professional, personal, business, and repair services	3,235	7.0	3,363	7.2
General government (including armed forces)	2,775	6.0	5,630	12.1

(continued)

TABLE I-1 (*concluded*)

Industry	1948		1963	
	Employment (thousands)	Percentage of U.S. Total	Employment (thousands)	Percentage of U.S. Total
Agriculture, forestry, and fishing	7,012	12.0	4,725	6.8
Mining	1,021	1.7	654	.9
Construction	3,262	5.6	4,305	6.2
Manufacturing	15,468	26.4	16,767	24.2
Transportation	3,000	5.1	2,546	3.7
Communications and public utilities	1,281	2.2	1,461	2.1
Government enterprise	720	1.2	987	1.4
Wholesale trade	2,712	4.6	3,391	4.9
Retail trade	8,597	14.7	10,537	15.2
Finance and insurance	1,349	2.3	2,437	3.5
Real estate	574	1.0	763	1.1
Households and institutions	3,051	5.2	4,316	6.2
Professional, personal, business, and repair services	4,449	7.6	6,182	8.9
General government (including armed forces)	6,080	10.4	10,336	14.9

Source: Office of Business Economics, *Survey of Current Business*, July 1962, July 1964; *U. S. Income and Output*, 1958; *National Income, 1954 Edition*.

perhaps cannot) improve as rapidly as in goods-producing industries. Doubts concerning the accuracy of the underlying data are widespread, however, and the analysis of the lag in service productivity, if it exists, has not been pushed very far.

Comparison of the goods and service sectors in the aggregate does reveal substantial difference in sector rates of growth of output per man; indeed, it is this differential rather than a drastic change in the composition of final output that appears to account for most of the shift of employment since 1929. However, when sector differences in rates of change of hours per man, quality of labor, and physical capital per worker are also taken into account, the productivity differential is much smaller than that based on output per man.

In this paper an attempt is made to obtain a better understanding of the factors affecting productivity by an examination of differences among detailed service industries. Such an approach, if applied with the caution that the imperfections in data and analytical techniques require, should permit some test of conclusions about productivity that have been reached on the basis of intersector comparisons and studies of productivity trends within manufacturing industries.

2

SCOPE, DEFINITIONS, AND SOURCES

THE LEVELS of employment in the service industries discussed in this paper are shown in Table I-2. They include all of retailing, divided into ten *retail trades,* and eight *services,* mostly of the "personal service" category. Together, they account for 17 per cent of total U.S. employment in 1963, 30 per cent of service sector employment,[1] and 51 per cent of the service sector excluding government, households, and institutions.

The industries chosen were those for which it was possible to obtain from available data reasonably comparable measures of output and input for selected years during the period 1939–63. Also, they are industries for which it is possible to calculate a measure of real output that is not based on labor input. It is widely recognized that where real output is estimated from labor input, as in government and much of the households and institutions sector, analysis of productivity change is scarcely possible.

A summary of the definitions, methods, and sources follows. Detailed information, as well as the actual data, are provided in the Appendix.

[1] The service sector is defined to include wholesale and retail trade; finance, insurance, and real estate; general government; and the services proper, including personal services, professional services, business services, and repair services. This somewhat arbitrary definition was chosen because of our interest in a group of industries that have not received much attention in the past from economists interested in productivity analysis. The boundary between service and goods production is very difficult to draw, and probably no division based on industrial classification would be completely satisfactory, because some workers employed in goods industries produce services and some in service industries produce goods. Note that Table I-2 is based on the *1963 Census of Business,* which became available in 1965. These figures are somewhat different from those in Table I-1, which are based on earlier data published by the Office of Business Economics.

A Statistical Analysis of Productivity

TABLE I-2

*Level of Employment and Percentage of Total U.S. Employment
in 18 Selected Service Industries, 1963*

Industry	Level of Employment (thousands)	Percentage of U.S. Total
Services		
Auto repair	414	.60
Barber shops	180	.26
Beauty shops	345	.50
Dry cleaning	268	.39
Hotels and motels	544	.78
Laundries	346	.50
Motion picture theaters	106	.15
Shoe repair	34	.05
Total	2,238	3.22
Retail trades		
Apparel stores	659	.95
Automobile dealers	860	1.24
Drug stores	365	.52
Eating and drinking places	1,933	2.78
Food stores	1,490	2.15
Furniture and appliances	459	.66
Gasoline stations	682	.98
General merchandise	1,434	2.06
Lumber dealers	466	.67
Other	870	1.25
Total	9,217	13.28
Total, 18 selected service industries	11,455	16.50

Source: U.S. Bureau of the Census, *1963 Census of Business*.
Coverage details are in the Appendix. U.S. employment is the number
of persons engaged in production from U.S. Department of Commerce,
Survey of Current Business, July 1964.

REAL OUTPUT

For the eight services, real output was defined as receipts in constant (1954) dollars. These were estimated from receipts in current dollars, as reported in the *Census of Business,* deflated by price indexes published by the Bureau of Labor Statistics (BLS).[2] To the extent that the price indexes take account of changes in the quality of services rendered, the real output measures do also.

For the ten retail trades, real output was assumed to be equal to the volume of sales of goods in real terms. This was estimated from receipts by type of store in current dollars, as reported in the *Census of Business,* deflated by price indexes prepared by David Schwartzman at the National Bureau. These indexes were based on detailed commodity components of the BLS consumer price index weighted by the importance of each commodity in each store type as reported in the *1948 Census of Business.* The BLS price indexes for retail sales of commodities do not attempt to allow for changes in quality of service rendered by retailers.

The real output measures for the eighteen industries should be considered only as approximations; they are not exactly equivalent either to the gross measures of physical output that are possible for some goods industries or to the estimates of real gross product originating that would be obtained through separate deflation of outputs and inputs.

EMPLOYMENT

The basic employment concept used is "persons engaged" as defined by the Office of Business Economics of the U.S. Department of Commerce. This is estimated from *Census of Business* data on employment and payrolls, with part-time wage and salary employees converted to full-time equivalents by assuming that their share of total wage and salary employment is equal to their share of total payroll. In addition to wage and salary workers, persons engaged includes self-employed proprietors, as reported in the *Census of Business,* all of whom are counted as employed full-time.

The estimates of the number of self-employed may be subject to con-

---

[2] Prices for hotels and motels were obtained from Horwath and Horwath, *Hotel Operations in 1963.*

siderable error because it is difficult to obtain complete coverage of numerous small firms and because the Bureau of the Census definitions of the minimum-sized firm to be included have varied from one census to another. Some attempt was made to adjust for changes in coverage (see the Appendix). Also, it is some comfort to note that the number of self-employed reported in the *Census of Business* for 1948 corresponds closely to the number reported in the *Census of Population* for 1950 for the eighteen industries.

The importance of obtaining an accurate count of the self-employed is considerable; they account for a significant fraction of total employment in many of the service industries, as may be seen in Table I-3. The employment estimates for these industries are probably not as reliable as those that can be obtained for manufacturing and other industries in which the self-employed play a much less important role.

Doubts may arise concerning the accuracy of the figures on self-employment, but the situation with respect to unpaid family workers is far worse. The *Census of Business* does not regularly report the number of such workers, and no attempt was made in this paper to include them in the measure of total employment. Some data for the eighteen service industries reported in the *1948 Census of Business* indicate that unpaid family workers (adjusted to full-time equivalents) amounted to about 8 per cent of total employment. The *Census of Population* for 1950, on the other hand, presents figures showing that unpaid family workers accounted for less than 2 per cent of employment in these industries.[3]

LABOR INPUT

Industry trends in effective labor input may diverge from trends in employment (full-time equivalents) because of differences in rates of change in hours per full-time worker or in the quality of labor as reflected in intelligence, strength, training, and so on. In the study of productivity, it is useful to have a measure of labor input that does

[3] The exclusion of unpaid family workers probably biases the estimates of the growth of output per man downward, because paid employment probably rose more rapidly than unpaid employment over the period studied. David Schwartzman, in the study of productivity growth in distribution that he is preparing for the National Bureau, estimates that the annual rate of growth of output per man in retailing, 1929–58, would be raised .08 per cent if unpaid family workers were included.

TABLE I-3

*Number of Self-Employed as a Percentage of Total Employment
in 18 Service Industries, Selected Years, 1939-63*

Industry	1939	1948	1954	1958	1963
Services					
Auto repair	48.6	41.3	40.4	34.9	33.1
Barber shops	66.9	61.8	62.3	60.7	61.4
Beauty shops	47.4	47.8	46.6	46.7	44.8
Dry cleaning	37.9	24.4	24.4	23.6	22.1
Hotels and motels	10.4	12.2	12.3	14.1	11.6
Laundries	8.2	10.2	9.2	10.0	12.8
Motion picture theaters	5.8	5.0	6.1	7.7	7.0
Shoe repair	71.9	69.1	68.4	64.8	65.2
Retail trades					
Apparel stores	19.5	16.0	16.1	15.3	13.8
Automobile dealers	11.7	11.2	10.2	10.7	9.0
Drug stores	22.1	17.2	17.1	14.8	12.4
Eating and drinking places	29.3	23.9	23.7	21.7	16.9
Food stores	44.8	38.2	32.1	27.2	21.6
Furniture and appliances	17.7	18.6	23.5	22.7	20.8
Gasoline stations	52.0	44.1	39.3	36.0	31.2
General merchandise	8.8	5.4	6.3	6.6	3.2
Lumber dealers	21.8	16.9	19.5	20.2	16.5
Other	34.8	29.3	33.9	31.8	28.5

Source: U.S. Bureau of the Census, *Census of Business*. Coverage
details are in Appendix B.

more than simply "count heads," i.e., that tries to take into account
these other factors. Given certain assumptions, it is possible to estimate
industry *differentials* in rates of change of labor input from rates of
change in labor compensation. If we assume that the price of a composite unit of labor of a given quality changes at the same rate in all
branches of the economy, then the change in total labor compensation
in a particular industry relative to the change in some other industry
is equal to the relative rates of change of labor input in those two indus-

tries.[4] Labor compensation for wage and salary workers was calculated from payroll data in the *Census of Business*. Compensation per man for self-employed was assumed to be the same as for employees in the same industry.[5]

OUTPUT PER MAN

This is real output divided by employment.

OUTPUT PER UNIT OF LABOR INPUT

This is real output divided by labor input. Absolute percentage rates of change for this measure have not been calculated because of the way in which the relative percentage rates of change of labor input are estimated. Relative values were obtained and used to rank the industries.

OUTPUT PER UNIT OF TOTAL INPUT

If one is interested only in ranking the industries according to their relative rates of change of output per unit of total input, an estimate can be obtained for the eight services by using the reciprocal of the rates of change of price. The rationale is that under competitive conditions, rates of change of price of service industries that have very little material input will tend to be inversely correlated with the rates of change of productivity. The implicit assumption is that the price of a composite unit of total input changes at the same rate in all industries. This is an extension of the assumption underlying the calculation of relative rates of change of labor input.

ANNUAL PERCENTAGE RATES OF CHANGE

The average annual percentage rate of change between 1939 and 1963 for each variable is calculated by fitting a least-squares equation of the form $lnX = a + bT + u$ on observations for 1939, 1948, 1954, 1958,

---

[4] Note that this formulation does not require that a dollar's worth of compensation buy the same amount of labor input in all industries. There may be variations based on nonpecuniary factors, monopoly or monopsony power, and so on. The relative change in compensation will still be equal to the relative change in labor input, provided these other factors do not change differentially by industry over time.

[5] Analysis of annual earnings of self-employed and wage and salary workers in these industries, as reported in the *1960 Census of Population*, indicates that this procedure probably results in an underestimate of the level of self-employment earnings.

and 1963. The regression coefficient b yields the annual percentage rate of growth compounded continuously. The annual rates for 1948–63 are obtained in a similar fashion by omitting the observation for 1939. It should be noted that the percentage rate of change of a variable formed by dividing one variable by another (e.g., real output per man) is approximately equal to the percentage rate of change of the numerator minus the percentage rate of change of the donominator.

An alternative way of calculating average percentage rates of change would be to use the initial and terminal years only. The difference in results obtained from the two methods is slight in most instances, but there are several industries where differences of .2 to .3 percentage points per annum are observed. Use of all the observations appears to be preferable in order to minimize the influence of the cyclical position of the initial or terminal year, or the influence of random events or errors in the data for one of those years.

The question of cyclical effect as opposed to trend is most important for comparisons based on 1939 because the economy had not yet fully recovered from the Depression and the unemployment rate was 17.2 per cent. The years 1948, 1954, 1958, and 1963 were all at a much higher level of activity than 1939, although 1954 and 1958 were marked by mild recessions. The unemployment rates for the four years were 3.8, 5.6, 6.8, and 5.7 per cent respectively.

3

EMPIRICAL RESULTS

RATES OF CHANGE, 1939–63

TABLE I-4 presents average percentage rates of change for each of the eighteen service industries. Table I-5 gives comparable figures for the aggregates and permits comparison with manufacturing, the total goods and service sectors, and the total economy. These tables are more or less self-explanatory and only a few brief comments need be made.

Perhaps the first and the most important point is that sixteen of the eighteen industries show positive rates of change of output per man. Unless the real output rates of change are systematically and markedly biased upward, there appears to be no basis for assuming that productivity cannot or does not increase in service industries. However, Table I-5 does show that the rate of increase for the services and the retail trades as a group was not as rapid as for manufacturing, the total goods sector, or the total economy.

If service industries generally tend to show positive rates of change of output per man, a serious question arises concerning the practice of assuming a zero rate of change for government and other service industries for which no convenient method of estimating output, independently of employment, has yet been found. Why not assume some constant, positive rate of increase, e.g., 1 per cent per annum, instead? It could be argued that such a procedure would be no more arbitrary and perhaps more accurate. Alternatively, one could assume for such industries the same average rate of increase as is found for those service industries for which an independent measure of output is available.

In a similar vein, the practice of assuming no differences in output per man for service industries across countries at a given point in time

TABLE I-4

Average Annual Percentage Rates of Change, Output per Man and
Related Variables, 18 Selected Service Industries, 1939-63

Industry	Real Output per Man	Real Output	Employ- ment	Compen- sation per Man
Services				
Auto repair	3.32	7.14	3.82	5.06
Barber shops	.60	.60	.00	5.67
Beauty shops	1.69	4.08	2.39	5.37
Dry cleaning	2.47	4.41	1.94	4.75
Hotels and motels	.49	2.20	1.71	5.35
Laundries	1.42	2.36	.94	4.78
Motion picture theaters	-2.83	-3.28	-.45	2.98
Shoe repair	1.16	-2.07	-3.23	4.77
Retail trades				
Apparel stores	.99	2.86	1.87	4.17
Automobile dealers	2.09	4.82	2.73	5.19
Drug stores	2.68	4.71	2.03	5.29
Eating and drinking places	-.18	2.30	2.48	5.31
Food stores	2.44	3.62	1.18	5.32
Furniture and appliances	2.88	5.37	2.49	4.88
Gasoline stations	3.25	5.25	2.00	5.08
General merchandise	1.40	3.53	2.13	4.38
Lumber dealers	1.21	3.07	1.86	4.99
Other	2.09	4.11	2.02	4.63

Source: Appendix B.

TABLE I-5

Average Annual Percentage Rates of Change, Output per Man and Related Variables, Industry Groups and Total Economy, 1939-63

	Real Output per Man	Real Output	Employ- ment	Compen- sation per Man
8 Services, total	1.14	2.68	1.54	5.07
10 Retail trades, total	1.63	3.67	2.04	4.90
18 Selected service industries, total	1.52	3.45	1.93	4.96
Manufacturing, total	2.26	4.22	1.96	6.32
Service sector, total	1.45	3.75	2.30	5.62
Goods sector, total	3.03	3.94	.91	6.83
Total economy	2.23	3.84	1.61	6.22

Source: Appendix B.

must be questioned. Is it not likely that some of the same factors that have contributed to increases in output per man in service industries in the United States over time might also be contributing to international differences in output per man at a given time?

A second point to be noted is the tremendous diversity of experience among the eighteen service industries. In one-third of the cases, output per man actually grew more rapidly than in the total economy. The range of variation for output and employment was also very great; only compensation per man tended to change at similar rates in the various industries.

RATES OF CHANGE, 1948–63

Tables I-6 and I-7 present the rates of change for the 1948–63 period. Output per man in manufacturing shows a higher rate of increase for this period, as do half of the retail trades, but the services all show higher rates for 1939–63. A tentative explanation is that *cyclical* fluctuations in output per man are more important in services, where

TABLE I-6

*Average Annual Percentage Rates of Change, Output per Man and
Related Variables, 18 Selected Service Industries, 1948-63*

Industry	Real Output per Man	Real Output	Employ- ment	Compen- sation per Man
Services				
Auto repair	1.85	5.78	3.93	· 3.27
Barber shops	.19	1.48	1.29	3.48
Beauty shops	1.54	6.76	5.22	3.34
Dry cleaning	1.65	.90	−.75	3.02
Hotels and motels	−.68	.86	1.54	3.19
Laundries	−.03	.86	.89	2.16
Motion picture theaters	−3.40	−6.46	−3.06	1.93
Shoe repair	1.16	−2.84	−4.00	3.03
Retail trades				
Apparel stores	1.62	2.06	.44	2.81
Automobile dealers	1.91	3.28	1.37	3.57
Drug stores	2.15	3.58	1.43	4.19
Eating and drinking places	.12	1.63	1.51	2.80
Food stores	2.75	3.58	.83	3.08
Furniture and appliances	3.38	3.40	.02	3.51
Gasoline stations	1.92	4.95	3.03	3.27
General merchandise	2.32	3.80	1.48	2.68
Lumber dealers	1.09	.18	−.91	3.59
Other	1.00	2.78	1.78	3.21

Source: Appendix B.

TABLE I-7

Average Annual Percentage Rates of Change, Output per Man and
Related Variables, Industry Groups and Total Economy, 1948-63

	Real Output per Man	Real Output	Employment	Compensation per Man
8 Services, total	.21	1.66	1.45	3.08
10 Retail trades, total	1.72	2.93	1.21	3.05
18 Selected service industries, total	1.41	2.65	1.24	3.07
Manufacturing, total	2.60	3.04	.44	4.86
Service sector, total	1.23	3.52	2.29	4.25
Goods sector, total	3.07	2.96	-.11	4.92
Total economy	2.14	3.23	1.09	4.54

Source: Appendix B.

employment is relatively insensitive to changes in demand and output.[6]
We again observe tremendous diversity among the eighteen industries
in rates of growth of all the variables except compensation per man.

Tables I-8 and I-9 present seventeen service industries,[7] ranked according to the various measures of output, input, and productivity.
Table I-10 shows the correlations between the rankings for 1939–63
and 1948–63. Most of these correlations are significantly different
from zero; this is not surprising considering the fact that there is a
great deal of overlap between these two periods. The correlations are
sufficiently below 1.00, however, to indicate that the inclusion or exclusion of 1939 can make a substantial difference, especially for the retail trades.

[6] See Victor R. Fuchs, *The Growing Importance of the Service Industries,* Occasional Paper 96, New York, National Bureau of Economic Research, 1965, pp. 45–51.
[7] "Other retail trade" is omitted from the rankings because it is a miscellaneous
category of questionable significance for economic analyses across industries.

Empirical Results

INTERINDUSTRY DIFFERENCES IN RATES OF CHANGE OF OUTPUT PER MAN

Given the substantial variation among service industries in rates of change of output per man, it is of interest to see whether the same pattern of variation can be found in some of the other variables, i.e., whether rates of change are correlated across industries.

The relationship between industry rates of growth and output per man is of particular interest. Many previous studies have found a significant positive correlation between these two variables.[8] The explanation of the relationship usually runs in two opposite directions—from productivity change to industry growth, and from industry growth to productivity. The first argument is that rapid productivity growth leads to lower prices which stimulate demand and output. The alternative argument is that changes in income or taste that increase demand and output permit economies of scale and other efficiencies which show up as higher productivity.

These previous studies have mostly been confined to or dominated by manufacturing industries. When this relationship was tested across ten major industry groups in the United States, no correlation between growth and productivity could be observed.[9] In this paper the hypothesis is tested across the seventeen service industries.

Tables I-11 and I-12 show the coefficients of rank correlation for every combination of variables. Correlations between output per man (O/E) and output (O) and employment (E) are the ones to be considered first. Either output or employment can be used to measure industry rates of growth; therefore, we must look at both sets of correlations. The correlation with output tends to be biased upward, and the reverse is true of employment.[10]

The coefficients shown in Tables I-11 and I-12 tend to support the

8 See, for example, Solomon Fabricant, *Employment in Manufacturing, 1899–1939*, New York, NBER, 1942, pp. 88, 146; John W. Kendrick, *Productivity Trends in the United States*, Princeton University Press for NBER, 1961, pp. 207–216; W. E. G. Salter, *Productivity and Technical Change*, Cambridge, Eng., 1960, p. 123.

9 Fuchs, *Productivity Trends*, p. 17.

10 Whenever a correlation coefficient is calculated between one variable and another which is based in part on the first, the danger of spurious correlation arises. To the extent that there are errors in the observations, these errors alone would tend to produce a positive or negative correlation, depending upon the position of the variable in numerator or denominator on both sides of the equation.

TABLE I-8

Rankings of 17 Selected Service Industries, Average Annual Percentage Rates of Change of Output per Man and Related Variables, 1939–63

Industry	Real Output per Man	Real Output per Unit of Labor Input	Real Output	Employment	Compensation per Man	Real Output per Unit of Total Input[a] (8 services only)
Auto repair	17	17	17	17	9	7
Gasoline stations	16	16	15	10	10	
Furniture and appliances	15	15	16	15	7	
Drug stores	14	13	13	11	12	
Dry cleaning	13	14	12	9	4	8
Food stores	12	12	10	5	14	
Automobile dealers	11	10	14	16	11	
Beauty shops	10	6	11	13	16	6
Laundries	9	8	6	4	6	5
General merchandise	8	11	9	12	3	
Lumber dealers	7	5	8	7	8	
Shoe repair	6	7	2	1	5	3
Apparel stores	5	9	7	8	2	
Barber shops	4	3	3	3	17	1
Hotels and motels	3	4	4	6	15	2
Eating and drinking places	2	2	5	14	13	
Motion picture theaters	1	1	1	2	1	4

Source: Table 4 and Appendix B.
[a]Based on the reciprocal of the rate of change of price.

TABLE 1-9

Rankings of 17 Selected Service Industries, Average Annual Percentage Rates of
Change of Output per Man and Related Variables, 1948-63

Industry	Real Output per Man	Real Output per Unit of Labor Input	Real Output	Employment	Compensation per Man	Real Output per Unit of Total Input[a] (8 services only)
Furniture and appliances	17	17	11	5	14	
Food stores	16	16	12.5	7	8	
General merchandise	15	15	14	12	3	
Drug stores	14	7	12.5	11	17	
Gasoline stations	13	13	15	15	10.5	
Automobile dealers	12	10	10	10	15	5
Auto repair	11	11	16	16	10.5	8
Dry cleaning	10	12	6	4	6	
Apparel stores	9	14	9	6	5	
Beauty shops	8	9	17	17	12	7
Shoe repair	7	8	2	1	7	6
Lumber dealers	6	5	3	3	16	
Barber shops	5	3	7	9	13	1
Eating and drinking places	4	4	8	13	4	
Laundries	3	6	4.5	8	2	4
Hotels and motels	2	2	4.5	14	9	2
Motion picture theaters	1	1	1	2	1	3

Source: Table 6 and Appendix B.
[a]Based on the reciprocal of the change of price.

TABLE I-10

Coefficients of Rank Correlation Between Average Annual
Percentage Rates of Change, 1939-63 and 1948-63, of
Output per Man and Related Variables,
Selected Service Industries

	17 Selected Service Industries	8 Services	9 Retail Trades
Real output per man	.77	.93	.72
Real output per unit of labor input	.79	.86	.58
Real output	.75	.76	.58
Employment	.58	.81	.25
Compensation per man	.58	.90	.20
Real output per unit of total input	n.a.	.81	n.a.

Source: Tables 8 and 9.

Note: Minimum values of rank correlation coefficients for various levels of statistical significance (two-tailed test):

α	$N = 8$	$N = 9$	$N = 10$	$N = 25$
.10	.64	.58	.56	.34
.05	.73	.68	.65	.40
.01	.86	.82	.79	.53

hypothesis of a positive correlation between growth and productivity. Table I-13 indicates that the relationship found among the seventeen service industries is of the same order of magnitude as that found by other investigators for manufacturing industries.

One way of circumventing the problem of spurious correlation between output per man and output, or between output per man and employment, is to fit least-squares regression lines directly to two equations relating changes in output and changes in employment. In one equation, output is treated as dependent upon employment; in the other equation, the relationship is reversed. If there is no correlation between industry rates of growth (measured by output or employment) and industry rates of change of output per man, the slope of the regression line between output and employment should equal unity. Regression lines with slopes greater than unity indicate a positive correlation. Slopes smaller than unity indicate a negative relationship.[11]

The regression lines for Charts I-1 and I-2 are as follows:

1939–63
$$O = .813 + 1.435E \qquad \bar{R}^2 = .727$$
$$\quad (.469) \quad (.217)$$
$$E = -.032 + .519O$$
$$\quad (.309) \quad (.078)$$

1948–63
$$O = .944 + 1.245E \qquad \bar{R}^2 = .768$$
$$\quad (.396) \quad (.169)$$
$$E = -.411 + .629O$$
$$\quad (.313) \quad (.086)$$

The slopes of the lines on the charts when employment is dependent are the reciprocals of the regression coefficients.

Both the rank correlations and the regression slopes indicate that the relation between growth and productivity was stronger for 1939–63 than for 1948–63. This probably reflects a cyclical relation between growth and productivity in addition to the secular one.

The finding of a positive relation between industry rates of growth and changes in productivity raises an interesting question about pro-

---

[11] Cf. Fabricant, *Employment in Manufacturing*, p. 87.

TABLE I-11

Coefficients of Rank Correlation, Average Annual Percentage Rates of Change (1939-63)
of Output per Man and Related Variables, Across Selected Service Industries

		Real Output per Man	Real Output per Unit of Labor Input	Real Output	Employment	Compensation per Man	Real Output per Unit of Total Input
Real output per man	(1)		.94	.93	.54	.06	
	(2)		.90	.90	.74	.07	.81
	(3)		.97	.93	.07	.12	
Real output per unit of labor input	(1)			.87	.50	-.15	
	(2)			.81	.57	-.14	.74
	(3)			.87	.03	.00	
Real output	(1)				.79	.10	
	(2)				.93	.21	.76
	(3)				.33	.02	
Employment	(1)					.10	
	(2)					.33	.67
	(3)					-.06	
Compensation per man	(1)						
	(2)						-.38
	(3)						

Source: Table 8.
(1) Across 17 selected service industries.
(2) Across 8 services.
(3) Across 9 retail trades.

TABLE I-12

Coefficients of Rank Correlation, Average Annual Percentage Rates of Change (1948-63) of Output per Man and Related Variables, Across Selected Service Industries

		Real Output per Man	Real Output per Unit of Labor Input	Real Output	Employment	Compensation per Man	Real Output per Unit of Total Input
Real output per man	(1)		.88	.70	.13	.38	
	(2)		.95	.71	.33	.43	.69
	(3)		.85	.69	-.10	.04	
Real output per unit of labor input	(1)			.71	.03	.07	
	(2)			.60	.21	.21	.83
	(3)			.51	-.25	-.26	
Real output	(1)				.73	.31	
	(2)				.84	.78	.26
	(3)				.55	-.13	
Employment	(1)					.18	
	(2)					.69	-.05
	(3)					-.38	
Compensation per man	(1)						
	(2)						-.14
	(3)						

Source: Table 9.
(1) Across 17 selected service industries.
(2) Across 8 services.
(3) Across 9 retail trades.

TABLE I-13

*Summary of Coefficients of Rank Correlation Between Rates of
Change of Output per Man and Output and
Employment Across Industries*

	Output per Man and	
	Output	Employment
1. U.S. 1939-63—17 service industries	.93	.54
2. U.S. 1948-63—17 service industries	.70	.13
3. U.S. 1899-1937—56 manufacturing industries	.73	.31
4. U.S. 1899-1953—33 industry groups	.64[a]	.33[a]
5. U.S. 1899-1954—80 manufacturing industries	.67[b]	.33[c]
6. U.K. 1924-50—28 manufacturing industries	.83	.57
7. U.S. 1929-61—10 major industry groups	-.01	-.84

Source by Columns: 1, Table 11; 2, Table 12; 3, Fabricant,
Employment in Manufacturing; 4 and 5, Kendrick, *Productivity Trends
in the U.S.;* 6, Salter, *Productivity and Technical Change;* 7, Fuchs,
Productivity Trends.

[a]Based on output per unit of total factor input.
[b]Based on output per adjusted man-hour.
[c]Based on output per man-hour.

ductivity trends in those service industries not included in the present
study.[12] As can be seen in Table I-14, the excluded industries had, on
average, much faster rates of growth of employment than did the seventeen included industries. If we were to assume that the relationships
shown in Charts I-1 and I-2 between growth of output and growth of employment extended to the excluded industries, we would have to con-
clude that output per man in those industries grew much more rapidly
than in the seventeen industries covered in the present study. Present
measures of real gross national product do not yield that conclusion,
but they are based for the most part on arbitrary assumptions about
real output, including the assumption that labor productivity never
changes. No widely acceptable alternative measure of real output for
the excluded industries is available.

[12] I am grateful to Edward F. Denison for calling this question to my attention.

The results shown in Tables I-11 and I-12 parallel those reported for manufacturing in one other respect, namely, the absence of any correlation between changes in output per man and changes in compensation per man. This result would appear to refute the hypothesis that differential changes in the quality of labor can make a significant contribution to the explanation of differential changes in output per man in these industries. On the other hand, there have been very large differences in rates of change of compensation per man between the service industries and manufacturing. This indicates that a differential change in labor quality may explain part of the differential change in output per man between manufacturing and the service industries.

One other set of correlations that was run tests the relation between changes in output per man and changes in the percentage of employment accounted for by self-employed. It has been argued that large numbers of the self-employed are not really very active and have very low productivity.[13] Their alternative to self-employment may be unemployment. One would expect, therefore, that industries which showed a large absolute decline in the percentage of employment accounted for by self-employed might show large increases in output per man. The coefficients of rank correlation shown in Table I-15 provide some slight support for this hypothesis, particularly with respect to the eight services. The same table also shows the correlations between changes in the self-employment percentage and percentage rates of change of output and employment. There is apparently some intercorrelation among all these variables, and much more work needs to be done before any conclusions concerning causality would be warranted.

This brief look at some individual service industries suggests that a much more intensive examination of a few industries might produce very interesting results. The statistical analysis presented in this paper has resulted in some tentative conclusions concerning the relation between productivity, growth, labor quality, and other variables. Through an intensive case study, it might be possible to discover just how these interrelations develop in specific industries and to obtain

---

[13] Edward F. Denison, "Improved Allocation of Labor as a Source of Higher European Growth Rates," in Michael J. Brennan (ed.), *Patterns of Market Behavior*, Providence, 1965.

CHART I-1

*Relation Between Average Annual Percentage Rates of
Change of Real Output and Employment, 17 Selected
Service Industries, 1939–63*

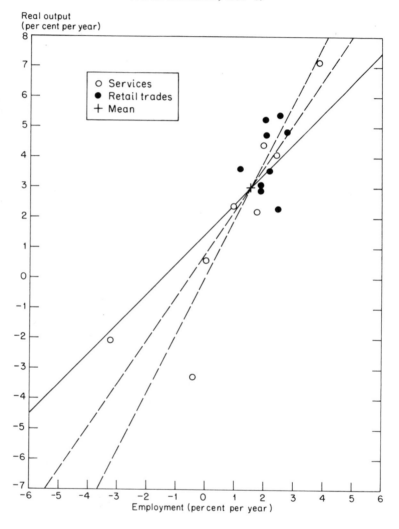

Real output
(per cent per year)

CHART I-2

*Relation Between Average Annual Percentage Rates of
Change of Real Output and Employment, 17 Selected
Service Industries, 1948–63*

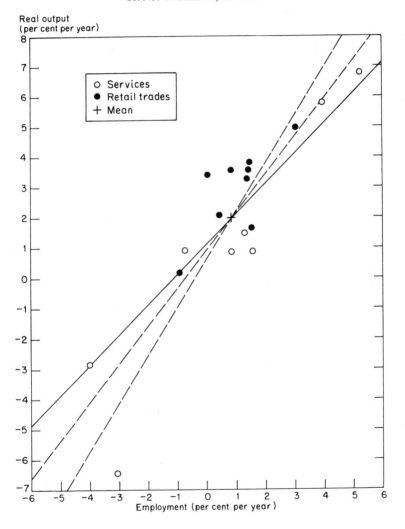

TABLE I-14

Comparison of Annual Rates of Change of Employment of 21 Excluded Service Industries with 17 Selected Service Industries, 1939-63
(per cent per annum)

Industry	1939-63	1948-63
Federal general government, military	8.64	4.12
Engineering and other professional services, n.e.c.	6.20	5.78
Business services, n.e.c.	5.77	5.79
Federal general government, civilian	4.80	1.56
Finance, n.e.c.	4.66	6.78
Commercial and trade schools and employment agencies	4.51	2.76
Nonprofit membership organizations, n.e.c.	4.20	3.22
Medical and other health services	4.17	4.48
Banking	3.84	3.84
Educational services, n.e.c.	3.60	3.89
State and local general government, public education	3.57	4.74
Insurance carriers	3.22	3.30
Insurance agents and combination offices	2.99	3.51
Miscellaneous repair services and hand trades	2.87	1.14
State and local general government, nonschool except work relief	2.83	3.34
Wholesale trade	2.32	1.49
Amusement and recreation except motion pictures	2.13	1.46
Security and commodity brokers, dealers, and exchanges	1.95	4.67
Real estate	1.81	1.90
Legal services	1.06	2.42
Private households	−1.27	−.18
Median of 21 excluded industries	3.57	3.34
Median of 17 selected services	1.87	1.29

Source: U.S. Office of Business Economics, *Survey of Current Business*, July 1964, Table VI-16; *U.S. Income and Output,* Table VI-16; *National Income, 1954 edition,* Table 28.

Note: For excluded industries, rates of change were computed between terminal years.

TABLE I-15

*Coefficients of Rank Correlation Between Change in
Self-Employment as Percentage of Total Employment
and Rate of Change of Output per Man,
Output and Employment*

		1939-63	1948-63
ΔS : O/E	17 service industries	-.36	-.45
	8 services	-.60	-.78
	9 retail trades	-.05	-.04
ΔS : O	17 service industries	-.29	-.12
	8 services	-.43	-.29
	9 retail trades	.25	.57
ΔS : E	17 service industries	-.57	-.43
	8 services	-.43	-.26
	9 retail trades	-.40	-.63

Source: Tables 3, 8, and 9.
Note: ΔS = Percentage self-employed in initial year minus percentage self-employed in terminal year. O, E, O/E = Average annual percentage rate of change of real output, employment, and real output per man.

an understanding of the process of productivity change at the level of the producing unit. Jean Wilburn's study (Part II) uses the contrast between the barber and beauty shop industries as a point of departure, and develops in detail answers to many of the questions that have been raised in this study.

PROBLEMS IN THE MEASUREMENT OF OUTPUT AND
PRODUCTIVITY IN THE SERVICE INDUSTRIES

IN APPRAISING the preceding results, it is well to recall that the measures of real output used can be considered only as approximations. Attempts to measure output and productivity in these and other service industries encounter conceptual and statistical problems which, if not unknown in the commodity-producing industries, take on a new form and increased importance that warrant some discussion.

RETAIL TRADES

The procedure followed in this paper and elsewhere of using the real volume of goods sold as a measure of retail trade output is open to a number of objections; there are many aspects of retailing that may vary over time or cross-sectionally. These include the following:

1. Terms of sale: credit, delivery, guarantees, replacement of parts, repairs and services, return privileges, etc.
2. Amenities provided to the customer: heating, air-conditioning, lighting, music, rest rooms, etc.
3. Convenience: location with respect to homes, places of work, and other stores, availability of parking facilities, store hours
4. Aids to customer choice: variety of merchandise, displays, "test drives," "home demonstrations," "try-on" privileges
5. Sales personnel: intelligence, information, courtesy, attention, etc.
6. Demands on customer: time and effort required to accomplish purchase
7. Size of transaction

One important source of difficulty is that shifts in the sales of the identical commodity from one type of retailer to another will affect the measure of productivity in different ways depending upon what assumptions are made. The problem may be seen clearly by means of a numerical example. In the example that follows, store type A represents an "old-style" full-line retailer, and type B a modern supermarket or low-markup retailer.

Store Type	Wholesale Price	Margin	Retail Price	Quantity	Sales
		PERIOD 1			
A	$1.00	$.50	$1.50	80	120
B	1.00	.30	1.30	20	26
				100	146
		PERIOD 2			
A	1.00	.50	1.50	20	30
B	1.00	.30	1.30	80	104
				100	134

According to present methods of measuring real output in retailing in the United States, the index of real output would be 91.8 (i.e., 134 ÷ 146) because the price index used to deflate sales would be unchanged from period 1 to period 2. Some economists would regard this as an overstatement of the change in real output in retailing. If the gross margins of the two store types can be regarded as measuring real differences in the services rendered by the two types of retailers, then the real output index should be 73.9 (i.e., 34 ÷ 46). Others would argue that the index should be 100, on the grounds that the same quantity of goods is being sold by retailers and that the lower margin represents a more efficient way of providing the same function. As can be seen, the present technique provides a result which is intermediate between the two extreme positions.

Change in the size of transaction is another difficult item to deal with conceptually. Suppose that all other aspects of the sale remain unchanged, but the customer now buys in each transaction twice as much as before. Shall we say that real output in retailing is twice as great as before? Some have argued that because an increase in the size of the transaction normally does not require a proportionate increase in inputs, the volume of real goods should not be used as the measure of real output. It has been suggested that the number of transactions be used, or at least considered, in determining real output in retailing.[14]

One difficulty with this line of reasoning is that it is not applied in measuring real output in other industries, such as manufacturing. Businessmen and economists have known for a long time that productivity is often positively related to the "length of the run." But rarely, if ever, does anyone adjust a manufacturing output index based on volume of goods produced in order to allow for changes in the "length of run."

[14] See Margaret Hall and Don Knapp, "Productivity in Distribution with Particular Reference to the Measurement of Output," *Productivity Measurement Review*, February 1957.

In retailing, the size of the transaction corresponds to the "length of the run," and there would seem to be little reason for treating this industry differently from others. Unless output is redefined in all industries, it seems more reasonable to try to identify what portion of the observed change in output per man in retailing can be attributed to change in the size of transaction.

My colleague, David Schwartzman, believes that differences in transaction size in food stores (and possibly other retail trades) explain a large part of differences in output per man. Margaret Hall appears to have reached the same conclusion. One test of this hypothesis would be to determine whether stores attempt to raise the average size of transaction through price concessions or other inducements.

The following notes on some of the individual retail trades provide some rough alternative measures of real output and compare them with the deflated sales indexes that have been used in this paper. Some of these alternatives serve as a check on the quality of the data; others involve a different concept of real output.

AUTOMOBILE DEALERS

A typical transaction in this industry consists of the sale of one car or one truck. The number of such sales may change radically from the deflated value of sales, as shown in the following figures.[15] The explanation for the differ-

1958 = 100	Deflated Sales	Number of New Cars and Trucks Sold [a]
1939	39.5	69.9
1948	77.8	102.9
1954	103.8	128.5
1958	100.0	100.0
1963	133.3	177.2

ences probably lies in changes in the proportion of low-priced, medium-priced, and expensive cars sold. One way of approaching this problem of measurement would be to look at the retail margins realized on cars in different price ranges. If the percentage margins are typically the same, regardless of price range, then the use of deflated sales as a measure of real output without regard to the number of cars sold would seem to be justified.

DRUG STORES

There seems to be a very close correspondence between deflated sales of drug stores and the total number of prescriptions filled. The index for indus-

---

[15] Sources for all of the series presented in this section are given in footnote 16.

trial production of drugs, soap, and toiletries seems to rise more rapidly than either of the other series. It may be that sales of these commodities have been increasing at a rapid rate in retail stores other than drug stores.

1958 = 100	Deflated Sales	Number of Prescriptions [b]	Industrial Production of Drugs, Soap, and Toiletries [c]
1939	37.9	32.3	n.a.
1948	71.2	69.8	45.2
1954	84.5	80.4	68.9
1958	100.0	100.0	100.0
1963	121.3	122.5	141.2

FOOD STORES

Changes in deflated sales of food stores have closely paralleled changes in industrial production of food in the postwar period. The average size of transaction has apparently been rising markedly as people tend to shop less frequently. There would be some increase attributable to higher incomes even if the frequency of shopping was unchanged.

1954 = 100	Deflated Sales	Industrial Production of Food [c]	Number of Transactions [d]
1948	77.8	86.4	n.a.
1954	100.0	100.0	100.0
1958	115.2	110.4	n.a.
1963	132.8	129.8	87.0

GASOLINE STATIONS

Gas stations are another type of retail outlet where the size of transaction may be of considerable importance. Casual observation suggests that productivity is much greater when pumping fifteen gallons into one tank than when servicing three cars for five gallons each. Transaction size has probably increased over time as gas tanks have become larger and incomes have risen. The following data seem relevant.

1958 = 100	Deflated Sales	Number of Privately Owned Cars, Trucks, and Buses [a]	Number of Vehicle Miles Traveled [a]	Gallons of Motor Fuel Consumed [a]	Size of Gasoline Tank (Ford) [e]	Replacement Production of Tires and Batteries [a]
1939	35.0	45.4	42.8	38.8	70.0	53.8
1948	57.5	60.2	59.8	57.1	85.0	.83.1
1954	81.8	85.7	84.4	83.1	n.a.	85.2
1958	100.0	100.0	100.0	100.0	100.0	100.0
1963	120.3	121.0	120.0	114.0	100.0	126.7

GENERAL MERCHANDISE STORES

The average size of transactions has apparently risen in general merchandise stores also.

1958 = 100	Deflated Sales	Number of Transactions (3 ÷ 4)	Receipts in Current $ ᶠ	Average Sale in Department Stores in Current $ ᵍ
	(1)	(2)	(3)	(4)
1939	53.9	61.7	27.4	44.4
1948	74.4	78.5	72.4	92.3
1954	83.2	89.1	81.3	91.3
1958	100.0	100.0	100.0	100.0
1963	131.3	117.7	135.0	114.7

LUMBER DEALERS, ETC.

The following figures suggest either that lumber dealers are losing out to other forms of distribution or that the deflated sales figures for 1963 understate the real amount of goods passing through this type of retail outlet.

| 1958 = 100 | Deflated Sales | INDUSTRIAL PRODUCTION OF | | |
		Lumber and Products ᶜ	Construction Materials ᶜ	Farm Equipment ᶜ
1948	95.2	96.0	79.3	143.5
1954	98.6	104.2	92.5	107.3
1958	100.0	100.0	100.0	100.0
1963	97.4	113.9	123.1	128.0

SERVICES

Many of the general points that were made concerning output in retail trades also apply to the services. The attitude and skills of the person supplying the service, the amenities provided to the customer, and the demand made upon the customer's time are clearly factors that should be considered in measuring real output. The principal question in the case of services seems to be: How well does the price index capture the quality dimensions of output? Shifts in the composition of output within a census industry can also present problems, as indicated in the following two examples.

HOTELS AND MOTELS

The postwar period has witnessed a marked shift in the composition of this industry from hotels to motels. In 1948, motels accounted for less than 10 per cent of total industry employment. By 1963 the share in motels was one-third. Receipts per worker have typically been about 5 to 10 per cent higher in motels than in hotels; this shift therefore would tend to raise the rate of change of output per man as currently measured. A factor that probably has considerable effect on output per man is the occupancy rate. Between 1939 and 1948 this rate rose markedly, but since then it has declined. By 1963 it was almost down to the 1939 level.

1958 = 100	*Deflated Sales*	*Occupancy Rate* [h]
1939	63.2	87.0
1948	103.2	123.2
1954	92.7	n.a.
1958	100.0	100.0
1963	117.4	91.3

MOTION PICTURE THEATERS

One of the factors tending to raise measured output per man in motion picture theaters has been a shift from regular movie houses to drive-ins. In 1948 the latter accounted for only 3 per cent of the industry's employment, but by 1963 this percentage had grown to over 20 per cent. Receipts per worker have typically been 10 to 20 per cent higher in drive-ins than in regular theaters.[16]

[16] Sources for series presented in this section are:

[a] Automobile Manufacturers' Association, *Automobile Facts and Figures*, various issues.

[b] Number of prescriptions per store from Eli Lilly and Company, *The Lilly Digest*, 1961, 1963, multiplied by the number of establishments from the *Census of Business*.

[c] Board of Governors of the Federal Reserve System, *Industrial Production Indexes*, 1961–63, and *Industrial Production, 1957–1959 Base*.

[d] 1963, Progressive Grocer, *Progressive Grocer;* 1954, Cox, Reavis, *et al.*, *Distribution in a High Level Economy*, Englewood Cliffs, N.J., 1965.

[e] Ford Motor Company dealer.

[f] U.S. Bureau of the Census, *Census of Business*.

[g] National Retail Merchants Association, *Merchandising and Operating Results*, various issues. Department and specialty stores until 1948, department stores only subsequently. 1954 data estimated by assuming the 1954–56 change in the average sale of "owned" departments applied to all departments.

[h] Harris, Kerr, and Foster, *Trends in the Hotel-Motel Business, 1963*. Rate refers to both hotels and motels.

THIS APPENDIX is divided into two sections, one for the eighteen selected service industries and the other for the industry aggregates with which they are compared. The discussion of the industry classifications and a description of the variables is followed by a table containing the basic data.

SELECTED SERVICES

Industry Classification. Two types of adjustments were necessary to achieve comparability of industries over time. The first consisted of shifting detailed kinds of business between industries. This was necessary because of modifications in the industrial classification adopted by the Census Bureau. The other adjustment concerned the inclusion of units other than stores. Non-store retailers, which consist of mail-order houses, vending-machine operators, and house-to-house selling organizations, had to be allocated by kind of business, beginning in 1954, when they were first shown separately. Administrative offices, warehouses, and auxiliaries, also shown separately, were included in each year. The eighteen selected service industries as defined in this paper are described in the following paragraphs, and the Standard Industrial Classification codes used in the 1963 *Census of Business* are indicated.

Barber Shops (SIC 724)—barber shops.

Beauty Shops (SIC 723)—beauty shops and combination barber and beauty shops.

Laundries (SIC 7211, 7212, 7213, 7214, 7215)—power laundries, industrial laundries, linen supply, diaper service, self-service laundries, and self-service dry cleaning. (Self-service dry cleaning was included in laundries because separate information was not available prior to 1963.)

Dry Cleaning (SIC 7216, 7271)—cleaning and dyeing plants (except rug cleaning), and cleaning and pressing shops.

Shoe Repair (SIC 725)—shoe repair, shoeshine, and hat cleaning establishments.

Auto Repair (SIC 75)—auto repair shops, parking, auto and truck rentals, and auto laundries.

Motion Picture Theaters (SIC 783)—regular motion picture theaters and drive-ins.

Hotels and Motels (SIC 7011)—year-round hotels, seasonal hotels, motels, tourist courts, and motor hotels.

Lumber, Building Materials, Hardware, Farm Equipment Dealers (SIC 52)—lumber yards, building materials dealers, heating, plumbing equipment dealers, paint, glass, wallpaper stores, electrical supply stores, hardware stores, farm equipment dealers.

General-Merchandise Group Stores (SIC 53, excluding part of nonstore retailers)—department stores, limited-price variety stores, general-merchandise stores.

Food Stores (SIC 54)—groceries, delicatessens, meat markets, fish markets, fruit stores, vegetable markets, candy, nut, confectionery stores, dairy products stores, retail bakeries, egg and poultry stores.

Automotive Dealers (SIC 55, excluding 554)—passenger car dealers, tire, battery, accessory dealers, home and auto supply stores, aircraft, motorcycle, boat, and household trailer dealers. (Dealers primarily engaged in selling trucks are classified under wholesale trade.)

Gasoline Service Stations (SIC 554)—gasoline service stations.

Apparel, Accessory Stores (SIC 56)—men's, women's, and children's wear stores, custom tailors, specialty stores, furriers, family clothing stores, shoe stores.

Furniture, Home Furnishings, Equipment Stores (SIC 57)—furniture stores, floor-covering stores, drapery, curtain, upholstery stores, china, glassware, metalware stores, household appliance stores, radio and television stores, music stores.

Eating, Drinking Places (SIC 58)—restaurants, lunchrooms, cafeterias, refreshment places, caterers, drinking places (alcoholic beverages).

Drug Stores, Proprietary Stores (SIC 591)—drug stores, proprietary stores.

Other Retail Stores (SIC 59, excluding 591)—liquor stores, book stores, stationery stores, sporting goods stores, bicycle shops, farm and garden supply stores, jewelry stores, fuel and ice dealers, florists, cigar stores, news dealers, photographic supply stores, optical goods stores, etc.

CURRENT DOLLAR OUTPUT

Current dollar output is defined as receipts from customers for services rendered and merchandise sold, whether or not payment was received. Receipts of income from investments, rental of real estate, and similar items are excluded. Beginning in 1954, state and local sales taxes and federal excise taxes collected by the establishment and paid directly to a tax agency are included. The only exception to this is motion picture theaters, for which taxes are included, beginning in 1939. Sales of each of the ten retail trades were taken as the sum of each component kind of business. For total retail trade, output was derived by adding the margins (sales minus cost of goods sold) of the ten retail trades. The margins as a percentage of sales were derived from Internal Revenue Service tabulations for corporations in 1957, published in the *Statistics of Income . . . 1957–58, Corporation Income Tax Returns* and used for all years. It was determined that there were no significant differences between margins as a percentage of sales for corporations and all firms. The aggregation procedure is not sensitive to possible inaccuracies in the margin percentages.

PRICES

Price indexes for all of the eight services, except hotels, are components of the U.S. Bureau of Labor Statistics Consumer Price Index. For hotels and motels, the average room rate for hotels in large cities was taken from Horwath and Horwath, *Hotel Operations in 1963*, p. 21. The drawbacks to this measure are that it is affected by quality of room and extent of multiple occupancy.

For the ten retail trades, price indexes were computed largely from components of the Consumer Price Index. Components of the Wholesale Price Index and other sources were also used. For each kind of business an index was obtained by weighting components by the share of commodity sales in 1948 given in the *Census of Business*.

REAL OUTPUT

Real output was obtained by deflating current dollar output by the price indexes.

EMPLOYMENT

Employment is defined as the number of full-time equivalent wage and salary workers plus the number of proprietors. The number of proprietors in retail trade was adjusted for changes in coverage, as will be described. Proprietors were assumed to be full-time workers, as were employees in administrative offices, warehouses, and auxiliaries of retail stores. Wage and salary workers were converted into full-time equivalents for 1948, 1954, and 1958 by assuming that the average hourly earnings of part-time workers were the same as the average hourly earnings of full-time workers in the same industry. The number of workers working the full workweek was multiplied by the ratio of payroll of all wage and salary workers to payroll of full-time wage and salary workers. For 1939, the procedure was based on annual rather than weekly earnings, since payroll and employment data were available on an annual basis only. For 1963, the 1958 relation between the total number of wage and salary workers and the number of full-time equivalent wage and salary workers were used because the number of employees working the full workweek was not given. Because data on employees of administrative offices,

warehouses, and auxiliaries were not yet published, they were assumed to be
the same percentage of full-time equivalent wage and salary workers in 1963 as
in 1958. Unpaid family workers are not included.

COVERAGE ADJUSTMENT

In retail trade, some establishments with no paid employees were excluded
from coverage in the *Census of Business* if receipts for the year did not
exceed $500 in 1948, and $2,500 in 1954 and 1958. An adjustment was made
to include proprietors on the 1939 coverage basis. It was assumed that the
1948 ratio of the number of establishments with receipts of under $2,000
to the number with receipts of $2,000 to $5,000 equaled the 1939 ratio of the
number of establishments with receipts of under $1,000 to the number with
receipts of $1,000 to $2,500, i.e.,

$$\frac{\overset{1939}{\text{Under } \$1,000}}{\$1,000-\$2,500} = \frac{\overset{1948}{\text{Under } \$2,000}}{\$2,000-\$5,000}$$

It was further assumed that there was one proprietor in each establishment
added by the adjustment. The adjustments were made in such a way as
roughly to allow for changes in the price level. For 1954 and 1958 the ratio

$$\frac{\overset{1939}{\text{Under } \$1,250}}{\$1,250-\$2,500} = \frac{\overset{1954 \text{ and } 1958}{\text{Under } \$2,500}}{\$2,500-\$5,000}$$

was assumed. For 1963 no adjustment was made, since for the first time establishments not operated during the entire year were included if their receipts
were at an annual rate of $2,500 or more. The procedure used in 1963 is
probably comparable to the coverage adjustment in prior years.

The number of proprietors added by coverage adjustment are (in thou-
sands):

	1948	1954	1958
Apparel, accessory stores	1.0	3.1	2.9
Automotive dealers	.1	1.3	1.8
Drug stores, proprietary stores	—	.4	.3
Eating, drinking places	2.8	12.5	15.0
Food stores	2.8	12.6	12.2
Furniture, home furnishings, equipment stores	.9	4.8	5.4
Gasoline service stations	1.1	3.1	2.7
General merchandise group stores	.3	1.9	2.7
Lumber, building materials, hardware, farm equipment dealers	.4	2.1	2.8
Other retail stores	3.8	20.1	19.6

Note: These estimates probably improve the over-all estimates of employment, but
because of changing coverage, definition, and presentation, they are subject to considerable error.

The minimum-receipts sizes for services were $400 in 1948 and $1,000 thereafter. Because the limits were lower, a smaller proportion of proprietors was excluded than was excluded from trade. Moreover, reasonable estimates could not be derived from published class intervals of the receipts-size distributions by the procedure used for retail trade. For these reasons, no adjustment was made for service industries.

TOTAL LABOR INPUT

Total labor input is measured by payroll of all employees. Payroll for the entire year was used throughout. The payroll of proprietors was obtained by assuming that proprietors had the same average annual earnings as full-time wage and salary workers in the same industry. For 1963, payroll of administrative offices, warehouses, and auxiliaries was assumed to be the same percentage of total payroll as in 1958.

OTHER INDUSTRIES

Methods and sources of data for the total economy, goods sector, service sector, and manufacturing are described here. Goods includes agriculture, mining, construction, manufacturing, transportation, communications and public utilities, and government enterprise. The service sector includes wholesale and retail trade, finance, insurance and real estate; personal, professional, repair, and other services; and general government. Current- and constant-dollar output are the gross product series of the Department of Commerce published in the *Survey of Current Business* of September 1964 and October 1962. The Office of Business Economics obtains constant-dollar output generally by separately deflating inputs and output. Price indexes are obtained implicitly from the current- and constant-dollar measures. For 1939, real gross product in manufacturing and goods were based on data in John W. Kendrick, *Productivity Trends in the United States,* Princeton University Press for NBER, 1961. The 1939–48 changes in Kendrick's series were applied to the 1948 gross product estimates. Employment is the number of persons engaged in production, published in the *Survey of Current Business* of July 1962 and July 1964, and in *U.S. Income and Output* and *National Income, 1954 Edition.* For total labor input, total compensation was used. Proprietors were assumed to have the same average annual compensation as wage and salary workers in the same industry group. Data on number of full-time equivalent employees and compensation of employees from which the estimate of total compensation was made were obtained from the same sources as the number of persons engaged in production. The employment and compensation figures all relate to full-time equivalents. Unpaid family workers are not included.

TABLE I-B

Output and Input in Selected Service Industries, Sectors and Total Economy, Selected Years, 1939-63

	Current Output (millions of dollars)	Price Index (1954=100)	Real Output (millions of 1954 dollars)	Employment (thousands)	Labor Compensation (millions of dollars)
			AUTO REPAIR		
1939	441	57.6	766	166.0	199
1948	1,561	79.6	1,961	246.2	605
1954	2,223	100.0	2,223	244.9	818
1958	3,853	111.9	3,443	378.2	1,313
1963	5,444	122.4	4,448	414.4	1,698
			BARBER SHOPS		
1939	231	39.9	579	186.3	169
1948	404	75.8	533	155.2	330
1954	552	100.0	552	147.3	417
1958	783	122.3	640	183.7	555
1963	907	139.5	650	180.3	658
			BEAUTY SHOPS		
1939	250	50.2	498	190.3	156
1948	434	92.0	472	163.3	293
1954	654	100.0	654	168.0	411
1958	1,028	113.8	903	246.4	642
1963	1,618	125.7	1,287	345.2	1,037

(continued)

TABLE I-B (continued)

	Current Output (millions of dollars)	Price Index (1954=100)	Real Output (millions of 1954 dollars)	Employment (thousands)	Labor Compensation (millions of dollars)
DRY CLEANING					
1939	323	63.9	505	169.4	163
1948	1,128	86.6	1,303	303.7	587
1954	1,497	100.0	1,497	314.1	750
1958	1,671	110.5	1,512	311.8	862
1963	1,765	118.1	1,494	268.1	807
HOTELS AND MOTELS					
1939	900	46.1	1,952	360.0	276
1948	2,368	74.2	3,191	444.3	778
1954	2,862	100.0	2,862	440.2	988
1958	3,644	118.0	3,088	524.8	1,277
1963	4,667	128.7	3,626	544.2	1,553
LAUNDRIES					
1939	528	52.7	1,002	281.7	264
1948	1,323	80.2	1,650	304.9	705
1954	1,605	100.0	1,605	329.2	800
1958	1,943	114.0	1,704	345.5	946
1963	2,493	133.1	1,873	346.5	1,102

(continued)

TABLE I-B (continued)

	Current Output (millions of dollars)	Price Index (1954=100)	Real Output (millions of 1954 dollars)	Employment (thousands)	Labor Compensation (millions of dollars)
MOTION PICTURE THEATERS					
1939	803	52.4	1,532	116.8	140
1948	1,614	85.8	1,881	170.2	319
1954	1,407	100.0	1,407	144.9	309
1958	1,172	116.9	1,003	134.9	294
1963	1,063	146.3	727	105.7	269
SHOE REPAIR					
1939	119	45.2	263	72.3	65
1948	219	88.2	248	64.1	118
1954	202	100.0	202	43.3	100
1958	232	115.4	201	44.7	105
1963	208	132.5	157	33.5	100
APPAREL, ACCESSORY STORES					
1939	3,259	49.2	6,628	421.3	558
1948	9,803	101.1	9,692	625.6	1,507
1954	11,214	100.0	11,214	648.8	1,900
1958	12,706	103.2	12,311	689.1	2,168
1963	14,204	108.2	13,129	658.8	2,446

(continued)

TABLE I-B (continued)

	Current Output (millions of dollars)	Price Index (1954 = 100)	Real Output (millions of 1954 dollars)	Employment (thousands)	Labor Compensation (millions of dollars)
		AUTOMOTIVE DEALERS			
1939	5,549	48.8	11,373	435.9	646
1948	20,104	89.6	22,432	695.0	2,111
1954	29,918	100.0	29,918	775.1	3,127
1958	31,824	110.4	28,833	794.5	3,416
1963	45,402	118.2	38,408	859.5	4,550
		DRUG STORES, PROPRIETARY STORES			
1939	1,562	66.2	2,360	225.4	236
1948	4,014	90.7	4,428	300.6	607
1954	5,252	100.0	5,252	316.5	846
1958	6,779	109.0	6,218	361.4	1,079
1963	8,487	112.6	7,537	364.6	1,402
		EATING, DRINKING PLACES			
1939	3,527	41.6	8,482	1,046.0	711
1948	10,683	92.4	11,560	1,570.2	2,579
1954	13,101	100.0	13,101	1,600.0	3,332
1958	15,201	110.0	13,818	1,834.8	3,901
1963	18,412	124.5	14,785	1,932.7	4,949

(continued)

TABLE I-B (continued)

	Current Output (millions of dollars)	Price Index (1954=100)	Real Output (millions of 1954 dollars)	Employment (thousands)	Labor Compensation (millions of dollars)
		FOOD STORES			
1939	9,560	41.4	23,075	1,134.6	1,267
1948	29,438	93.0	31,654	1,329.9	3,521
1954	40,646	100.0	40,646	1,395.7	4,438
1958	49,693	106.1	46,823	1,492.6	5,147
1963	58,021	107.5	53,983	1,490.1	6,349
		FURNITURE, HOME FURNISHINGS, EQUIPMENT STORES			
1939	1,798	54.5	3,300	255.0	351
1948	7,252	100.6	7,210	466.5	1,228
1954	9,450	100.0	9,450	494.6	1,720
1958	10,481	97.4	10,765	517.2	1,923
1963	11,481	95.9	11,972	459.4	2,085
		GASOLINE SERVICE STATIONS			
1939	2,822	61.5	4,592	445.4	427
1948	6,483	85.9	7,549	447.9	885
1954	10,744	100.0	10,744	516.8	1,393
1958	14,178	108.0	13,128	657.0	1,820
1963	17,760	112.5	15,788	682.1	2,256

(continued)

TABLE I-B (continued)

	Current Output (millions of dollars)	Price Index (1954=100)	Real Output (millions of 1954 dollars)	Employment (thousands)	Labor Compensation (millions of dollars)
	GENERAL MERCHANDISE GROUP STORES				
1939	6,475	51.9	12,478	849.1	983
1948	17,135	99.6	17,206	1,154.2	2,684
1954	19,241	100.0	19,241	1,234.8	3,216
1958	23,665	102.3	23,144	1,339.3	3,982
1963	31,937	105.1	30,381	1,433.9	4,956
	LUMBER, BUILDING MATERIALS, HARDWARE, FARM EQUIPMENT DEALERS				
1939	2,735	44.7	6,123	301.4	408
1948	11,152	86.4	12,906	543.7	1,441
1954	13,366	100.0	13,366	553.1	1,895
1958	14,720	108.6	13,556	553.7	2,103
1963	14,792	112.1	13,199	466.2	2,141
	OTHER RETAIL STORES				
1939	4,156	53.4	7,778	546.5	712
1948	12,930	92.2	14,025	682.6	1,660
1954	16,628	100.0	16,628	737.3	2,407
1958	19,872	105.4	18,856	863.4	2,860
1963	23,258	109.8	21,178	869.7	3,519

(continued)

TABLE I-B (continued)

	Current Output (billions of dollars)	Price Index (1954=100)	Real Output (billions of 1954 dollars)	Employment (thousands)	Labor Compensation (billions of dollars)
		EIGHT SERVICES			
1939	3.60	50.7	7.10	1,543	1.43
1948	9.05	80.5	11.24	1,852	3.74
1954	11.00	100.0	11.00	1,832	4.59
1958	14.33	114.7	12.49	2,170	5.99
1963	18.17	127.4	14.26	2,238	7.22
		TEN RETAIL TRADES			
1939	11.20	48.3	23.20	5,661	6.30
1948	34.26	93.9	36.48	7,816	18.22
1954	43.80	100.0	43.80	8,273	24.27
1958	51.71	105.9	48.82	9,103	28.40
1963	62.75	110.6	56.72	9,217	34.65
		EIGHTEEN SELECTED SERVICE INDUSTRIES			
1939	14.80	48.8	30.30	7,204	7.73
1948	43.31	90.8	47.72	9,668	21.98
1954	54.80	100.0	54.80	10,105	28.86
1958	66.04	107.7	61.31	11,273	34.39
1963	80.92	114.0	70.98	11,455	41.87

(continued)

TABLE I-B (continued)

	Current Output (billions of dollars)	Price Index (1954=100)	Real Output (billions of 1954 dollars)	Employment (millions)	Labor Compensation (billions of dollars)
MANUFACTURING					
1939	n.a.	n.a.	47.9	10.09	14.5
1948	73.1	85.0	86.0	15.47	49.2
1954	103.8	100.0	103.8	16.25	71.9
1958	120.9	110.2	109.7	15.72	84.7
1963	160.4	115.8	138.5	16.77	110.2
SERVICES					
1939	n.a.	n.a.	95.3	21.97	28.4
1948	115.9	83.4	139.0	26.81	72.7
1954	172.5	100.0	172.5	31.56	108.1
1958	221.3	113.4	195.1	33.94	142.5
1963	299.2	126.2	237.0	37.96	193.0
GOODS					
1939	n.a.	n.a.	93.7	24.64	28.0
1948	142.4	89.7	158.7	31.76	90.4
1954	189.1	100.0	189.1	31.78	125.6
1958	221.1	108.3	204.2	30.88	148.2
1963	281.6	112.4	250.5	31.45	187.1

(continued)

TABLE I-B (concluded)

	Current Output (billions of dollars)	Price Index (1954=100)	Real Output (billions of 1954 dollars)	Employment (millions)	Labor Compensation (billions of dollars)
			TOTAL ECONOMY		
1939	90.2	48.1	189.0	46.60	56.3
1948	258.4	88.5	297.8	58.58	163.2
1954	361.5	100.0	361.5	63.35	233.7
1958	442.4	110.8	399.3	64.82	290.7
1963	580.7	118.5	487.6	69.41	380.2

Source: See text of this appendix.

II

A CONTRAST IN PRODUCTIVITY TRENDS

WITHIN PERSONAL SERVICES: THE BARBER

AND BEAUTY SHOP INDUSTRIES

Jean Alexander Wilburn

4

INTRODUCTION

AMONG the industries providing personal services, barber and beauty shops rank second with respect to annual receipts and employment.[1] According to the most recent *Census of Business,* in 1963 their receipts amounted to $2.5 billion out of $9.2 billion, and these shops engaged half a million people of the 1.4 million working in the personal services.

Because they share many common characteristics, barber and beauty shops are frequently treated as one industry. First, their function is essentially similar, both being engaged primarily in grooming the hair. Second, the size of establishment in both cases is referred to as "typically small." Furthermore, most of these establishments are unincorporated. Of 106,000 establishments engaged in barbering in 1963, 99,000 were individual proprietorships and only 44,000 had any paid employees. Out of 152,000 beauty salons, 136,000 were individual proprietorships and only 74,000 had one or more paid employees.[2]

Both businesses are heavily labor-intensive. When barbers are paid on a straight commission basis, their earnings can run as high as 75 per cent of their receipts; the percentage for beauticians is somewhat less.[3] Cost of materials used by beauty salons is estimated at about 10

[1] The *1963 Census of Business* includes under personal services, in addition to barber and beauty shops, laundries (including cleaning and dyeing plants), photo studios, shoe repair, funeral services, pressing establishments (including garment repair and storage), and miscellaneous personal services. Laundries rank first, with receipts of $4.0 billion and personnel of about 600,000.

[2] *Census of Population,* 1930, 1940, 1950 editions; *Occupational Outlook Handbook,* 1963–64 edition, Bureau of Labor Statistics, pp. 317, 319; *1963 Census of Business,* Selected Services, Legal Form of Organization, BC 63-SS5, Table 1, and Employment Size, BC 63-SS3, Table 1.

[3] Bureau of Labor Statistics, *Monthly Labor Review,* June 1939, pp. 1287–1299; also, *Occupational Outlook Handbook,* Bulletin 1215, 1957, pp. 212–214.

per cent of receipts.[4] The figure is probably lower for barbers. Finally, capital investment in machinery and furniture for either type of establishment is low. To equip a one-chair beauty shop cost about $2,000 in 1955, and only $5,000 for a four-booth shop. In 1960, a one-chair barber shop was estimated to cost only $1,500. These figures can be considerably reduced by the use of secondhand equipment.[5]

In view of these similarities, it might appear appropriate for this study not to distinguish between barber and beauty shops and to treat them as one industry. From the standpoint of productivity, however, the differences between the two are more noteworthy than the likenesses. In fact, the contrast between them is so sharp as to suggest that more can be learned by a comparison of one with the other than through an attempt to understand them in the context of the service sector as a whole, or by juxtaposition with some other industry in the goods or service sector.

Their divergent performance is clearly reflected in Table II-1, which shows the price index of each industry and the index of real output per full-time worker for the benchmark years 1939, 1948, and 1963.[6] The more rapidly rising prices of barber services—which increased from an index of 52.6 in 1939 to 183.9 in 1963, as contrasted with 54.6 in 1939 to 136.6 in 1963 for beauticians—suggest a lower increase in productivity in that industry. This is substantiated by the productivity figures.[7]

Chart II-1 shows graphically the same index numbers of real output per worker as well as indexes of real output and employment. The relation between changes in output, employment, and productivity can be seen in two ways. During the years 1939–48, real output and employment dropped slightly in both industries, accompanied by increases in productivity for each industry of about the same order of magnitude,

[4] Interview with L. A. Freiberg, executive secretary, National Hairdressers' and Cosmetology Association, Inc.

[5] Department of Labor, *Employment Opportunities for Women in Beauty Services,* Women's Bureau Bulletin No. 260, 1965; *Occupational Outlook Handbook,* Bureau of Labor Statistics Bulletin No. 1300, 1961.

[6] Productivity figures for the decade 1929–39 have not been included because barber and beauty shops were not included in the *Census of Business* until 1933. The depression years are not suitable as benchmarks against which to measure changes in productivity.

[7] A gross measure of output per worker is used rather than value added because the cost of material is very small and has changed little over time.

TABLE II-1

Indexes of Prices and Productivity in Barber Shops and Beauty Shops, 1939, 1948, 1963
(1948=100)

Year	Prices		Real Output per Man[a]	
	Barbers	Beauticians	Barbers	Beauticians
1939	52.6	54.6	91.5	90.6
1948	100.0	100.0	100.0	100.0
1963	183.9	136.6	106.4	129.0

Source: Bureau of Labor Statistics, component part of the Consumer Price Index, *Census of Business*, 1939, 1948, 1963.

[a]For 1939 and 1948, employment is in terms of full-time equivalents. Part-time employees were reduced to full-time equivalents by assuming that hourly earnings were the same for part-time workers and therefore that hours worked were proportionate to earnings. For 1963, the 1958 ratio of full-time equivalent employees to the number of full-time plus part-time employees was assumed to apply. Real output was calculated by deflating each industry's receipts from the *Census of Business* by the component part of the Consumer Price Index.

1.0 per cent per annum for the barber and 1.1 for the beautician. Between 1948 and 1963, beauty shops had a very large increase in output, employment, and productivity. In contrast, the barber's increase in output and employment was modest and the rise in productivity small.

Over the twenty-five year period, output, employment, and productivity all rose substantially in beauty shops. Employment among barbers, on the other hand, remained almost constant, while output rose a little and productivity increases were small. These comparisons tend to agree with Victor Fuchs' study, which found a high degree of correlation between changes in output, productivity, and employment.[8]

Table II-2 shows that the average annual rate of increase in real output per full-time worker is considerably higher for the beautician than for the barber: 1.5 contrasted with .6 for the latter.[9] The performance

[8] See pp. 19–23.

[9] Output per man-hour is not included in this table because data on hours are not strictly comparable over time. Data for 1940 refer to wage and salary workers only. In addition, there is wide variation in time allotted for lunch and dinner. Often a meal is eaten in the shop as opportunity provides.

CHART II-1

*Indexes of Output, Employment, and Productivity, Barber and
Beauty Shops, 1939–63*

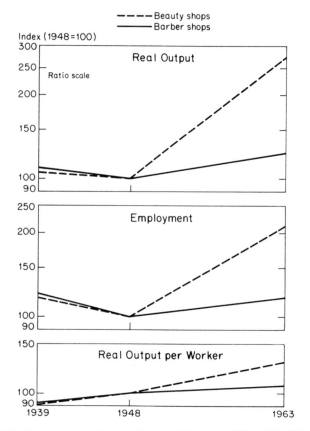

Source: U.S. Bureau of the Census, *Census of Business,* 1939, 1948, 1963.

in the period 1948–63 is primarily responsible for the marked long-run
differences: 1.8 per cent for the beautician and only .3 per cent for the
barber. During the same period, barber prices rose from an index of
100.0 to 183.9, but beauty-shop prices rose to only 136.6. Table II-2
indicates that although neither industry matched the performance
of the total economy in growth of real output per worker for any
period, beauty shops performed much better than barber shops.

Comparisons of changes in output per unit of total factor input

TABLE II-2

Average Annual Rates of Change of Productivity of Barber Shops, Beauty Shops, and the Total Economy, 1939–58

	Real Output per Worker[a]			Real Output per Worker Relative to Total Economy			Real Output per Unit of Total Factor Input[b] Relative to Total Economy		
	1939–48	1948–63	1939–63	1939–48	1948–63	1939–63	1939–48	1948–63	1939–63
Barber shops	.99	.33	.64	−1.35	−2.03	−1.71	−.35	−2.15	−1.52
Beauty shops	1.10	1.80	1.53	−1.24	−.56	−.82	+.05	−.13	−.07
Total economy	2.34	2.36	2.35	—	—	—	—	—	—

[a]Real receipts per full-time equivalent employee.

[b]Computed indirectly through the use of price indexes. Differences in price movements reflect differences in productivity changes unless there are unequal changes in the price of a unit of factor input. For a full description of the method used, see Edward F. Denison, *The Sources of Economic Growth in the United States and the Alternatives Before Us*, Committee for Economic Development, Supplementary Paper No. 13, New York, 1962, pp. 217–219.

(based on relative price changes) yield similar results.[10] Again, the beauty shop surpasses the barber shop over each period, 1948–63 showing the largest increase. The beauty shop's performance is about the same as the total economy's in both periods.

The plan of this study has been influenced by the dramatic difference in performance between the barber and beauty shops. It will treat them as two distinct industries and compare one with the other with respect to those factors which traditionally have been thought to bear on productivity, such as capital investment, hours worked, the quality of labor, technological change, and changes in demand.

Emphasis will be placed on comparison of productivity changes over the long-run period 1939–63,[11] rather than on analysis of each decade separately, for two reasons. First, average annual rates of change over the long period are likely to be more accurate than those for shorter periods. Second, when a factor influencing productivity has been operating over both decades, it is not always possible to be certain to what extent each decade has felt the impact.

New earnings data, providing information not previously available, and leading to some surprising results, will then be analyzed along with certain factors that appear to have special relevance for productivity in these industries. In conclusion, implications of the results of this study for other service-industry studies will be indicated and some suggestions will be offered for further research on the two industries.

---

[10] The method of computing changes in output per unit of total factor input differs from that for output per worker, but the methods are not completely independent since both involve the use of the same price indexes. Consistency between both sets of figures, therefore, does not offer proof but only support of the accuracy of the measures.

[11] Some data are not available for 1963. In that case, either 1939–58 or 1940–60 is considered the long-run period.

5

BACKGROUND

DURING the first decade of the twentieth century, two advances in technology, bearing revolutionary but dramatically opposed implications for the two industries, were introduced, and during the years that followed they won increasing acceptance. Widespread adoption of the safety razor not only ended the expansion of the relatively large and ancient service of barbering but precipitated an actual decline. Acceptance of the permanent-wave machine, on the other hand, marked the beginning of rapid expansion for the then insignificant and little-known industry of cosmetology.

The number of barbers began to decline following 1910, shortly after the safety razor was introduced. As late as 1920 the safety razor was priced at $3.65, but it dropped to the popular price of $1 the following year when the patent expired. During the 1930's the electric shaver was introduced; and by 1947 it had annual sales of $2.5 million.[12] Yet as late as 1933 barber shops ranked first among all the service industries covered by the *Census of Business* in employment and receipts. Receipts for 1963 in constant dollars are about one-fifth lower than they were estimated to have been in 1929. Formerly, the barber's function was a fairly complicated one, for he was called upon to perform a wide variety of services. The demand for these services has fallen away to such an extent, however, that the barber's work today is stereotyped and essentially limited to one service—haircutting.

Beauty services traditionally were a function of the home. Fashion change, technology, and the movement of women into the labor force have encouraged the growth of the industry, with significant implica-

[12] George J. Stigler, *Trends in Employment in the Service Industries*, Princeton University Press for NBER, 1956, p. 102.

tions for productivity. The permanent-wave machine, although long in existence, required the impetus of fashion change provided by bobbed hair in the 1920's to make it popular. Since then a continuous series of technological innovations has been supported by fashion changes. So successful has the interplay between the two been that more women now demand not only the beautician's services but a wider variety of them.

TRENDS IN RECEIPTS AND EMPLOYMENT

Table II-3 lends quantitative support to the foregoing generalizations. In 1929, barber shops were estimated to have had receipts over twice those of the beauty salons, whether measured in current or 1948 dollars. Both industries have increased their receipts in current dollars, but the beauty shops have done so at a much faster rate. Over the long run the receipts of barbers have tripled, and the beauty shops have had more than a tenfold increase. More informative is the per-

TABLE II-3

Receipts and Personal-Consumption Expenditures,
Current and Constant Dollars
($ million)

	1929[a]	1935	1939	1948	1958	1963
	CURRENT DOLLARS					
Barber shops	332	209	231	399	783	907
Beauty shops	159	192	250	434	1,028	1,618
	CONSTANT (1948) DOLLARS					
Barber shops	626	454	439	399	486	493
Beauty shops	286	399	458	434	831	1,184

Source: *National Income,* 1951, p. 192; *Census of Business,* 1935, 1939, 1948, 1958, 1963.

[a]Figures for 1929 are estimated receipts based on personal-consumption expenditures less 5 per cent for tips. See *National Income,* 1951, p. 111, for method of estimation. While these figures are not sufficiently reliable in absolute magnitude to serve as a base on which to calculate changes in productivity per annum, they are included here to show the trend in the two industries more clearly.

formance in constant (1948) dollars. Barber shops have declined from $626 million in 1929 to $493 million in 1963, while beauty shops have quadrupled from $285 million in the earlier period to $1,184 million in 1963.

Between 1939 and 1948, constant-dollar receipts fell in both industries. For barber shops this represented, in lesser magnitude, a continuation of the 1929–39 pattern of behavior. The receipts of beauty shops, however, had been increasing between 1929 and 1939, so that the 1939–48 drop reflects an interruption of the long-term trend. In the absence of any satisfactory explanation of this behavior, a question arises over the accuracy of the data, especially when Table II-4 is

TABLE II-4

Receipts and Personal-Consumption Expenditures, Current Dollars
($ million)

	1939	1948	1963
Census of Business receipts plus tips[a]	505	900	2,726
Office of Business Economics personal-consumption expenditures	518	1,030	2,818

Source: *Census of Business*, 1939, 1948, 1963; *Survey of Current Business*, November, 1965, pp. 20–21.

[a]Five per cent has been added for tips in 1939 and 8 per cent in later years, following the procedure used by the Office of Business Economics.

considered.[13] *Census of Business* receipts and Office of Business Economics personal-consumption expenditures for the combined industries agree except for 1948, the year in question.[14] In this year personal-

[13] The introduction and sale of home-permanent kits in the late 1940's may possibly be a cause of the fall in receipts. The Bureau of Labor Statistics, noting a drop in employment between 1939 and 1948, rejected this explanation, without indicating its reason for doing so. The *Census of Manufactures* for 1948 did not report the number of home permanents sold, nor would the manufacturer disclose the information. Whether the sale of home permanents influenced the 1948 figures significantly remains unanswered.

[14] The industries cannot be shown individually because the Office of Business Economics discontinued reporting them separately for the last benchmark year.

consumption expenditures are higher and might therefore be thought more appropriate to use. The Office of Business Economics, however, adjusted *Census of Business* figures upward to correct for enumerator misses. This could not be done for 1939 and has not as yet been done up to 1963. Because the concern is with consistency in measurement over time rather than accuracy at a point of time, *Census of Business* figures have been used rather than personal-consumption expenditures.

Not only have barber-shop real receipts declined but so has the number of barbers. Table II-5 shows that the number of barbers per 1,000 males decreased from 4.2 in 1930 to 2.0 in 1960, and that the total number fell from 261,096 to 179,670.[15]

In 1933, as well as ranking first among all service establishments in employment, number of establishments, and receipts, barber shops accounted for about 12 per cent of receipts, $204.3 million out of $1.7 billion. In relation to receipts of $811.4 million for the personal services only, barbering receipts accounted for 25 per cent. By 1963, services [16] had increased to $39.5 billion, but the barber-shop receipts had risen to only $906.6 million, representing about 2 per cent of the total. Personal services had risen to $9.2 billion, so that the barber, instead of accounting for 25 per cent of total receipts, is responsible for only 10 per cent.

Beauty salons, in contrast, have kept pace with the expansion of personal services. In 1933, when receipts were $116.8 million, they accounted for 14 per cent of personal-service receipts; in 1963, when receipts were $1,618 million, they accounted for 17 per cent. Meanwhile, the number of beauticians per 1,000 females has risen from 1.9 in 1930 to 3.4 in 1960.

RESTRICTIONS TO ENTRY

Over the years the interest of both economists and members of the legal profession has been attracted by the measures of control, such as licensing laws, found in the service trades and professions. The barber industry is the archetype of strong control, and has therefore frequently been singled out for analysis.

---

[15] These figures include proprietors and wage and salary workers, whether part or full time. A part-time worker is counted as one worker.

[16] Excluding hotels and places of amusement, which were not included in the 1933 figures.

TABLE II-5

Employment of Barbers and Beauticians, 1930–60

	Number of Barbers[a]	Barbers per 1,000 Males in Population	Number of Beauticians[a]	Beauticians per 1,000 Females in Population
1930	261,096[b]	4.20	113,194[b]	1.87
1940	209,259[c]	3.20	206,592[c]	3.18
1950	192,595[c]	2.63	189,870[c]	2.50
1960	179,670	2.03	305,858	3.36

Source: *Census of Population*, 1930, Vol. 5, Table 3; 1950, *U.S. Summary*, Table 125; 1960, Occupational Characteristics, Table 2.

[a]Males in the occupation group barber and beauticians are assumed to be barbers and females to be beauticians in 1930, 1940, and 1950. In 1960 the *Census of Population* provided separate information on employment in each occupation. These figures should be comparable with the figures for earlier years, since the percentage of males to females in each occupation has remained fairly constant over time.

[b]Gainful workers 10 years old and over.

[c]Employed persons 14 years old and over.

Control takes various forms—trade associations, unions, and state boards of barbers. The last named recommend and press for passage of legislation regulating wages, hours, prices, and the right to practice the occupation. These boards are typically composed entirely or mainly of practicing barbers appointed from the trade association and the union. Seldom is provision made for a member to be appointed from the public, even though the ostensible purpose of the board's existence is to protect the public welfare.

Attempts to restrict competition can be rigorous. Wisconsin, for example, created a statute effective June 28, 1961, which reads, "It is unlawful for any person to advertise a definite price for any barbering service by means of displaying a sign containing such prices so that the same is visible to persons outside the barber shop." [17] Similar laws had been enacted in 1942 by Rhode Island and in 1941 by Ohio.

There is wide variation among states in legislation bearing on the right to practice as a barber. All except New Jersey require some barber-school attendance; the number of hours required ranges from 900 to 2,000. Examination after graduation before the period of apprenticeship begins is customary; the fee for it is as high as $50 in some states and as low as none or $5 in others. The period of apprenticeship, during which earnings are restricted by law, ranges from six to thirty-six months. Following the apprenticeship is another examination costing from $5 to $50. A further barrier to entry is erected in some cases by refusing to give credit for out-of-state experience. Formal educational requirements, which exist in most states, range from eight through twelve years.[18]

Minimum-price legislation exists in some states, and prices are probably higher where this legislation exists.[19] The relation between the degree of unionization and barbers' wages has been studied, and an earlier work analyzed the effect of all barber legislation on prices.[20] These studies indicate that the supply of barbers has been limited and

[17] *Law Governing the Practice of Barbering,* State of Wisconsin, State Board of Health, Barber Division, insertion following page 6.

[18] *Research Report No. 3B, State Barber Laws,* National Association of Barber Schools, Inc., July 1, 1963.

[19] Simon Rottenberg, "The Economics of Occupational Licensing," in *Aspects of Labor Economics,* Princeton University Press for NBER, 1962, pp. 14–20.

[20] H. G. Lewis, *Unionism and Relative Wages in the United States,* Chicago, 1963, pp. 86–90; William F. Brown and Ralph Cassady, Jr., "Guild Pricing in the Service Trades," *Quarterly Journal of Economics,* February 1947, pp. 311–338.

their earnings and prices raised above the level that would obtain under more competitive conditions of demand and supply.

Control over beauty shops is less in evidence. There are licensing laws and a trade association for beauticians. The degree of unionization, however, is weak. Only 10 per cent of the membership of the Journeymen Barbers, Hairdressers, Cosmetologists, and Proprietors International Union of America is female. Eleven per cent of hairdressers are male, and only a fraction of them are union members.

Some comments on the effectiveness of controls will be made later after a discussion of the factors affecting productivity.

6

CONVENTIONAL FACTORS AFFECTING PRODUCTIVITY

CAPITAL investment per worker in barbering and hairdressing, as was previously indicated, is low. The *Census of Manufactures* figures for shipments of combined barber and beauty shop equipment give some indication of this. In constant 1948 dollars, shipments per worker were $34 in 1939, $67 in 1947, and $48 in 1958.[21] Capital investment per worker in barbering over time has remained fairly constant, whereas it may have dropped for beauticians.

In earlier years the heat permanent-wave machine cost several hundred dollars.[22] This machine has been replaced by a chemical process that involves only plastic curlers and lotions. Packages containing equipment for six individual permanents were sold at $6 per dozen in 1950.[23] Changes in rent over the long-run period cannot be estimated since no figures are available for earlier years. For 1960 the Internal Revenue Service reported combined barber and beauty shops as having paid rents amounting to 7.6 per cent of total receipts. Another source reported rents for 1962 as 6.3 per cent of sales.[24] If, then, rent is estimated at about 7 per cent, capital input would be somewhat less, since a portion of rent represents items such as management

---

[21] Current-dollar figures were deflated by the general-purpose machinery and equipment wholesale price index.

[22] *American Hairdresser*, January 1935, shows Nestle's permanent-wave machines ranging in price from $257 to $388 each. This magazine carries in July 1939 a Helene Curtis advertisement for a permanent-wave machine at $295.

[23] *Ibid.*, June 1950.

[24] *Statistics of Income*, 1960–61, p. 71; Accounting Corporation of America, *Mail-Me-Monday Barometer of Small Business, Yearbook, 1962*, p. 92.

expenses and real estate taxes. With amounts involved so small and remaining so nearly constant, or dropping, capital input cannot have had much bearing on changes in productivity in either industry.

HOURS

Table II-6 shows the average hours worked by full-time workers in 1940, 1950, and 1960. While the barber's hours have always been longer than the beautician's the reduction has been similar over time in the two industries and cannot be a significant factor in explaining differ-

TABLE II-6

Average Weekly Hours Worked,[a] *Employed Persons, 1940–60*

	1940[a]	1950	1960
Barbers[b]	53.0	50.1	48.4
Index	105.8	100.0	96.6
Beauticians[b]	47.0	44.6	44.2
Index	105.4	100.0	99.1

Source: *Census of Population,* 1940, 1950, 1960.

[a]*The Census of Population* for 1940 gives hours for wage and salary workers only. The number of hours worked in 1940 by employed persons was estimated on the assumption that the change in hours for employed persons, 1940–50, equals change in hours for wage and salary workers.

[b]Those working 35 hours or more.

ences in rates of change of output per worker. On the basis of change in hours alone, one would expect output per worker to rise more rapidly in barber shops than in beauty shops because the longer the workweek in the base-year period, the more likely it is that decreases in hours will be offset by increased output per man-hour.

It is a matter of historical interest that hours appear to have undergone a sharp reduction between 1930–40. Data on hours are not available from the 1930 *Census of Population;* however, statistics of the hours worked at the time by union barbers can be obtained from the Bureau of Labor Statistics analysis of the hours worked by unionized barbers in 63 cities of the United States.[25] The union membership represented in these cities was reported to be 26,960, or about 10 per cent of all barbers. The median number of hours per week out of 85 observations was 57⅔ within range limits of 46 to 69 hours. The interquartile range was from 55 to 62 hours per week.

A not too precise idea of hairdressers' hours in the early 1930's can be obtained from a survey made between December 1933 and April 1934 by the Department of Labor.[26] The survey covered four cities, Philadelphia, New Orleans, St. Louis, and Columbus. In shops with white employees, half the women worked over 48 hours. A report to the Industrial Commission to the Beauty Shop Minimum Wage Board of March 1938 quotes a previous study on beauty parlors in New York City which indicated the range of hours worked as from 45 to over 72 per week.[27] In 1936 the median hours were 49 per week, and by 1939 they had been reduced to 45.

QUALITY OF THE LABOR FORCE

Sex. Factors affecting the quality of the labor force differ in the two industries. The most obvious contrast is that of sex: barbers are predominantly male, 97.1 per cent; and cosmetologists predominantly female, 88.8 per cent.[28] The percentage has changed little over time. In 1939, women represented 3.8 per cent of the employees in barber shops, and 91.9 per cent of the employees in beauty salons.[29] Women today are probably more productive workers than they were in earlier periods because they have had more opportunity to gain experience.[30]

Education. No data on formal education are available for 1930; but from 1940 through 1960, barbers have had a markedly lower education than beauticians. From Table II-7 it can be seen that their education is also lower than that of both males and females in the total labor force. Beauticians' education has not only substantially exceeded that

---

[25] Department of Labor, Bureau of Labor Statistics, *Union Scales of Wages and Hours of Labor*, Bulletin H 515, May 15, 1929, pp. 325–327.

[26] *Employment Conditions in Beauty Shops*, Women's Bureau, Bulletin No. 133.

[27] New York State Department of Labor, Division of Women in Industry and Division of Junior Placement, *Employment Opportunities in Beauty Shops in New York City*, October 1931.

[28] *Census of Population, 1960*, p. 8.

[29] Stigler, *Employment in the Service Industries*, p. 10, n. 13.

[30] For a discussion of this point, see Denison, *Sources of Economic Growth*, p. 80.

TABLE II-7

Median Years of Formal Education Completed, 1940–60

	Barbers	Beauticians	Service Workers[a]		All Occupations	
			Male	Female	Male	Female
1940[b]	8.3	11.8	8.3	9.5	8.7	10.8
1950[b]	8.8	12.0	8.8	9.6	9.7	11.8
1960	9.2	12.1	9.7	10.2	11.1	12.1

Source: *Census of Population*, 1940, pp. 113, 114, 115; 1950, pp. 107, 113; and 1960, pp. 116, 121, 128.

[a]Excludes domestics.

[b]Barbers and beauticians are grouped together in the *Census of Population* for 1940 and 1950. Males have therefore been assumed to be barbers and females beauticians.

of all service workers but in 1940 and 1950 was superior to the education of females in all occupations.

It might be thought that the barber's educational differential is related to the number of foreign-born among barbers. However, as early as 1930, foreign-born barbers were only 30 per cent of the total and in 1960 only 18.6 per cent.[31]

The beautician's increase in formal education over time is too small to have affected productivity changes significantly. The barber now completes almost one more year of formal education than in 1940, which may have contributed to his small productivity increase.

The effect of vocational education on labor quality should also be considered. Over the years both industries have increased the variety of courses to be studied and the length of time spent in vocational school before taking the state examination. As these requirements were increasing, the service for which they were preparing the barber narrowed down to just one—haircutting. Yet the barber must often study such subjects as "scientific scalp and facial treatment for cosmetic purposes, use of creams, lotions, and other preparations in conjunction with galvanic, faradic, and high frequency electricity, ultra-violet radiation, vibratory appliances, barber shop management, ethics, salesmanship, standardized services, advanced haircutting and shaving techniques (including scientific finishing and artistic grooming), and professional courtesy." [32] It is difficult to believe that the average barber can utilize such elaborate preparation.

The beautician has had an increased number of skills to master, and the additional hours of vocational schooling and courses required have more immediate application.[33] Provision has been made for hairdressers to take courses that bring them up to date on new techniques when they return to the industry after an absence. Many more operators today are all-round operators than in 1936, if New York State can be used as a guide. In 1936, 63.1 per cent were all-round operators; whereas in 1956, 88 per cent were so classified according to studies made by that state's Department of Labor. This broadening of skills makes for increased flexibility in the use of operators in smaller shops.

---

[31] *Census of Population, 1930,* V, 84 and 113.

[32] Rottenberg, in *Aspects of Labor Economics,* p. 18.

[33] A visit to a large school of cosmetology (Queens Beauty School) revealed that instruction time was principally spent on those subjects which are essential for practicing cosmetology, e.g., hairsetting, cutting, tinting, manicuring.

Increased vocational education, then, as a factor explaining increases in productivity has more relevance for beauty than barber shops.

Age. Another quality of the labor force which bears on productivity is age. The distribution of barbers has so altered over the years as to increase the percentage at the least productive ages and decrease the percentage at the most productive ages. Table II-8 indicates that in 1938 earnings were highest between 25–34 and 35–44 years of age; between 1929 and 1958 the percentage of barbers in these groups dropped from 55.6 per cent to 34.8 per cent. Barbers 65 years and over had the poorest earnings, yet their percentage increased from 2.9 in 1930 to 13.3 in 1960. Moreover, earnings of barbers 55–64 years of age are also lower than at younger ages. In 1930 only 12.2 per cent were 55 years or older; today this figure has risen to 35 per cent.[34] The explanation for this shift seems to be that employment in the industry has declined absolutely.

In contrast, the percentage of beauticians has increased in those age groups where earnings are highest—45 to 64 years. In 1930 only 9.8 per cent were in this age group, but in 1960 28.6 per cent were represented there. At earlier ages, when earnings are lower, the percentage has been substantially reduced.

It is to be anticipated that the rapidly aging labor force contributes to lower productivity among barbers. The physical strain of standing with arms elevated above shoulder level can be very taxing, especially on busy days, when the position is maintained fairly continuously. Although beauticians other than manicurists stand, their arms are held at a more comfortable position. The physical slowing down of the barber as he ages cannot be compensated for in terms of better-quality performance. After cutting hair for a couple of years, the barber attains maximum proficiency, and additional years of practice do not yield improvements in performance. The beautician, on the other hand, has ample opportunity to improve the quality of her work with practice because the nature of the service is more varied and subtle. These improvements are then reflected in increased productivity and earnings.

[34] The question might be raised whether earnings figures for older barbers are too low because no distinction has been made between full- and part-time workers. Only 10 per cent of all barbers are part-time workers, however, so that it is unlikely that serious error would result from the failure to adjust for this factor.

TABLE II-8

Percentage Distribution and Median Earnings of Barbers and Beauticians by Age, 1930–60

Years	16–24	25–34	35–44	45–54	55–64	65+	55 Years and Over	Median Years
Barbers								
1930a	11.6b	26.6	29.0	19.4	9.3	2.9	12.2	37.8
1940c	4.9	20.4	28.2	26.4	14.8	5.4	20.2	43.4
1950c	4.8	15.1	21.9	26.6	21.6	10.1	31.7	47.6
1960d	6.9	17.2	17.6	23.5	21.7	13.3	35.0	48.1
Beauticians								
1930a	26.6b	37.1	23.9	8.0	1.8	.4	2.2	29.3
1940c	34.5	34.2	20.6	8.3	2.0	.4	2.4	28.5
1950c	16.3	34.2	29.7	13.9	4.7	1.0	5.7	34.3
1960d	15.6	20.3	33.2	20.7	7.9	2.3	10.2	38.7
Median Earnings, 1958e								
Barbers	$2,811	$4,157	$4,302	$3,951	$3,717	$2,096		
Beauticians	1,612	1,960	2,059	2,199	2,187	1,258		

Source: Census of Population, 1930, 1940, 1950, 1960.
aGainful workers.
b18–24 years. This row will not total 100 per cent since years 10–17 have been omitted.
cEmployed persons. Males are assumed to be barbers and females beauticians.
dEmployed persons. The two occupations are listed separately. Barbers are the sum of male and female barbers; the same is true of beauticians.
eExperienced civilian labor force.

TECHNOLOGY—BARBER SHOPS

A barber in the late 1920's could still devote his whole day exclusively to shaving, despite the introduction of the safety razor; but by 1939, the electric and safety razors combined had curtailed the number of shaves substantially, although shaving was still a significant part of the barber's service.[35] In 1947 a survey made in Los Angeles revealed a maximum of four shaves performed per day by any barber.[36] Today the figure is even less, some shops refusing to shave at all.

The fall in barber-shop shaves tended to reduce the demand for other services. When it was customary for men to visit a barber shop to be shaved three or four times a week, their hair was trimmed more frequently. At the slightest suggestion of shagginess of the hair at the back of the neck, the barber made a practice of calling the customer's attention to it by holding a mirror behind him. Usually the customer responded amenably to this suggestive selling and agreed to a trim.[37] During the 1920's many men did not shampoo their own hair, but turned to the barber for this service as well as for scalp and face massage.

The depression years witnessed a radical change. Men had good substitutes in the safety or electric razor for barber shaving services and they began using them in order to save money. Services complementary to shaving showed a similar decline. When the depression was over, the value of the time saved by shaving at home discouraged men from returning to their former pattern. The benefits of the most important technological innovation in barbering thus accrued not to the barber but to the household.

There have been other technological innovations in barbering, such as the electric clipper for haircutting. This has reduced the length of time required to cut a man's hair, especially in those shops that rely entirely on clippers. The quality of the cut is felt to be inferior by some men, however, so that many shops use scissors primarily. The lather for shaving sideburns is now produced by an electric machine

---

[35] Brown and Cassady, "Guild Pricing," p. 333; U.S. Department of Labor, *Job Descriptions for Domestic and Personal Service,* Washington, 1939. The technological changes that led to the substitution of household for market services may have been partly induced by changes in the costs of time.

[36] Brown and Cassady, "Guild Pricing," p. 333.

[37] Part of the cost of a haircut is the time spent going to and from the barber's. When a man had to go for a shave anyway, the real cost of a haircut was lowered.

rather than by hand, which has probably saved the barber a few minutes. No precise measure can be made of the effect on productivity of such devices, but they apparently have not had major impact. By far the most significant result of changes in barbering technology on productivity has been felt in the household and not in the industry.

TECHNOLOGY—BEAUTY SHOPS

Before 1920, beauty services were considered an expensive luxury by most women; they took care of their own hair. But the craze for bobbed hair in the 1920's caused an abrupt change. Women could not cut their own hair and they discovered that once it was cut, it needed special care to look attractive.[38] A permanent-wave machine had been on the market as early as the first decade of the century, but public acceptance of it did not come until the 1920's, when permanent waves became a complementary service to cutting the hair short.

During the 1930's some improvements were made to this machine. For example, a temperature of 350° F. was originally required for it to achieve its results. In 1935 the Frederics Company marketed a new spiral-type permanent-wave device which functioned properly at only 160°, and some time was saved by its use since it turned off automatically. In the first half of the 1940's the cold-wave permanent was discovered. Its popularity was by no means immediate, however. In 1945 the Helene Curtis cold wave was price-protected at $50. Demand was sharply limited, for not only was it too highly priced for popular consumption but the effectiveness of its results was controversial. The cold wave as it is known today was the result of a series of small technological improvements which were gradually developed since 1948. The full impact of these innovations was felt in the middle of the 1950's, at which time the average price had dropped to a range of from $7.70 in Scranton to $16.00 in Seattle.[39]

The operator saved a substantial amount of time through the use of instant neutralizers and faster processing lotions. In addition, she was freed to service other customers while the chemical reaction of the

---

[38] U.S. Department of Commerce, *Establishing and Operating a Beauty Shop,* Washington, 1946.

[39] Sources for this paragraph are *American Hairdresser,* January 1935 and January 1945, a summary provided by the Marketing Research Department of Helene Curtis Industries, Inc., January 7, 1964, and Bureau of Labor Statistics preliminary sample of permanent cold waves, 1955.

permanent was taking place. During the application of the older heat permanent, she had to stand continuously at the customer's chair because of the danger of scalp burning.

The impact of the cold wave on productivity is substantial, since it is estimated to have cut the labor time required for a permanent in half. Meanwhile, by the middle 1950's the demand for permanents had grown to the point where they represented 67 per cent of receipts of the beauty salon.[40]

A somewhat similar pattern of development characterized hair coloring. Clairol, the well-known tinting agent, was in existence as early as 1920, but demand was small. At that time the process had many limitations. It offered the consumer few colors, which were neither attractive nor sufficiently subtle to leave doubt that a person's hair was dyed. Between 1939 and 1949, Clairol began advertising a new coloring material noted for producing a "natural look." In the late 1940's and the 1950's many technological improvements were made which reduced the length of time required for the operator to perform the service. During the 1950's demand rose to the point where coloring represented 15 per cent of beauty-salon receipts.

It is in the last couple of years, however, that the response to changed techniques in coloring has been most dramatic. Patrons are normally introduced to coloring by a temporary color rinse which lasts four to six weeks. In the last year or two this type of product has been so perfected that it has wave-set properties and can be administered at the dressing table rather than at the sink, thus eliminating rinsing and saving time and effort. After experiencing these temporary rinses, the customer will frequently accept permanent hair coloring.[41] So successful has the approach been that today receipts from coloring are said to represent one-third of total salon receipts.

Hair dryers have been improved so as to decrease the length of time that a woman must remain under one to dry her hair after it has been set. The work of adjusting the temperature to the comfort of the individual has been transferred from the operator to the customer by simply putting the thermostat within easy grasp of the customer, rather than above her head or behind her.

[40] Interview with L. A. Freiberg of the National Hairdressers' and Cosmetology Association.
[41] Helene Curtis summary.

The innovations so far described have been those that have saved the operator time with no loss, but rather a gain, in the quality of the service performed, thus contributing directly to increased productivity. Another kind of technological innovation, however, does not necessarily save time directly. Colored nail enamel, facial packs, and various rinses are of this type. Beauty-shop suppliers develop such products and hope they will be accepted by the public. If the consumer does accept them, the result is to broaden the variety of services which the beauty shop must offer. This movement away from specialization would normally be considered a factor affecting productivity adversely. There is an offset, however, through the effect on demand.

The relation between the degree of specialization and productivity in both industries contrasts strangely. On the one hand, the barber, who has become more specialized through offering fewer services over the years, until today for the most part he offers only one—haircutting —has had a low rate of increase in productivity. On the other hand, a relatively high rate of increase has been achieved in cosmetology, which originally was highly specialized. The beautician used to perform mainly the "shampoo and set," but today she tints, rinses, sets, and permanent-waves the hair, manicures and pedicures the nails, tweezes the eyebrows, gives facials and massages, along with the selling and servicing of wigs.

SPECIALIZATION AND DEMAND

The probable explanation for this paradox lies in changes in demand. The total demand for the barber's services shrank to the point where specialization was of small benefit; i.e., demand for a variety of services shrank to a demand for only one service. There is little effect on the productivity of a barber who takes half as long as previously to cut a man's hair if the liberated time must be spent idly waiting for another customer. Consumer demand is now focused mainly on one service, the haircut, which takes about twenty minutes to perform today, in contrast to perhaps thirty minutes at earlier periods, when other services were also in demand. It would require a very precise and even flow of customer traffic, say, one man every twenty or twenty-five minutes, to keep the barber productive all day and therefore in a position to take advantage of quicker performance because of specialization. No such even flow of business exists, however, a factor which will be explored more fully a little later. When each customer demanded several services of the barber, there was less dependence on a precise and even flow of demand. If business was slow, the barber could help spread demand by suggesting additional services, such as a shampoo or massage, to the customers. On the other hand, if he was operating at a peak period, he could withhold any suggestive selling, merely shaving and cutting the hair of each customer.

This should not be interpreted to mean that no benefits from specialization have been felt by the barber. On those days when traffic is heavy and continuous, he obviously can process more customers, thereby adding to his measured productivity. No doubt part of the 1 per cent average annual rate of increase in real output per barber between 1939–48 can be attributed to this specialization, for it was during that decade that time devoted to shaving services dropped from a significant amount to virtually none.

In the beauty shop the adverse effect on measured productivity because of widening the variety of services has been offset by several factors. Attention was previously called to the percentage increase in the number of women who are all-round operators. In the small shop, employment of such personnel makes for greater flexibility in the distribution of work and leads to increased productivity. If the demand at the moment in a small shop is not for tinting services but is instead for a haircut, the tinter need not remain idle; she cuts the customer's hair. In the large shops, however, both increased demand and demand for a wider variety of services has had the effect of increasing specialization, which has helped productivity.

One further consideration relates to the nature of the demand itself. Increased demand for beauty-shop services may take different forms. One woman may come more often for the same service or a woman may demand more kinds of services. It is the latter demand, resulting in a wider variety, whose effect on productivity has been described as possibly adverse. Fortunately, however, an offsetting factor accompanies this form of demand. The woman who requests a variety of services usually does so at one sitting. The result can then be beneficial for the following reasons.

Associated with each customer is what might be called a setup time. If the customer is tardy, the operator often wastes time awaiting her arrival. Once the customer is in the shop, she first identifies herself and her appointment is verified. Then she removes her outerwear and dress and puts on a smock, sometimes assisted, sometimes not. She is next asigned to a particular operator and is directed to her chair. Obviously, if each customer came for only one service, the amount of unproductive setup time would be higher in relation to the more productive time of the operator.[42] When more than one service is requested, sometimes two can be performed at once. Finally, there is greater latitude and flexibility in planning and timing the work load. The advantages associated with the demand for a large quantity of services at one sitting rather than small amounts of services at discontinuous time periods are analogous to those benefits in the production of goods which accrue from one large order of $100,000 in contrast to 100 orders of $1,000 each.

During a recent National Bureau investigation of productivity in retail food stores, a similar situation was found by David Schwartzman.[43] Productivity in food stores was found to be influenced significantly by the size of the average transaction. Both the present study and Schwartzman's offer empirical evidence supporting the theoretical presentation of Armen Alchian, which emphasizes the advantages of planned larger batch or lot quantities of output over a period of time rather than planned rates of output.[44]

It appears, then, that there is justification for concluding that improved technology accompanied by increased demand has contributed to the beautician's improved productivity.

ECONOMIES OF SCALE

It was earlier pointed out that both barber and beauty shops are commonly referred to as "typically small." This characterization is appropriate if the two industries are compared with others in the economy. There are differences, however, between the two industries studied here. In 1958, barbering establishments with receipts of $50,000 or more accounted for only 5 per cent of total barber receipts, but beauty shops in the same category were responsible for 22 per cent of their

[42] It seems likely that the larger and more elaborate the shop, the greater the amount of setup time.

[43] The unpublished material on food stores is part of a larger work on productivity in retail establishments in which Schwartzman is now engaged.

[44] "Costs and Output," in *The Allocation of Economic Resources, Essays in Honor of Bernard Francis Haley,* Stanford, 1959.

total. Only 2 per cent of total barber receipts came from shops with annual sales of $100,000 or more, in contrast to about 11 per cent for beauty salons.[45]

These figures suggest that few benefits from economies of scale accrue to the barber. The effects on the beauty shop are less obvious. Table II-9 indicates that, at any point in time, the larger the establishment, the greater the receipts per worker. Attributing this to economies of scale is a doubtful interpretation, however, because average annual earnings also rise with size of establishment. Higher receipts per worker might be the result of better-quality labor in larger shops. Table II-10, last column, indicates some economies of scale, since there is a small rise in the ratio of receipts to payroll.

Labor quality might increase with size of shop for several reasons. Attention was called in the last section to the fact that the larger the shop, the greater the use of specialists, who receive higher wages than nonspecialists. In order to specialize in a particular field, such as hair styling or tinting, the operator takes postgraduate work at a beauty school, or sometimes an apprenticeship is served under a famous European or American operator. In such cases, improved quality takes the form of the ability to provide a more exciting and attractive hair style or color. Talent and training vary among specialists; the most competent are likely to go into the large prestige salons, where prices and earnings are high.

Large establishments, however, can also be very low-priced and highly competitive, the opposite of the large prestige salon. The physical volume of services performed is heavy and continuous. In these shops, the better quality of the specialist is evidenced by the speed and efficiency with which the customer is serviced.

Over the period 1939–58,[46] the larger the establishment, the smaller the increase in productivity. Presumably, demand has always been strong enough in the big shops to warrant employment of as large a number of full-time workers as are needed, or there would have been fewer. This is supported by the fact that the larger the establishment, the lower the percentage of part-time employees. Little increase in

---

[45] Census of Business, 1958, V, 2–28. The average beauty shop is somewhat larger than the average barber shop. There are more self-employed than wage and salary workers among barbers; the reverse is true of beauticians.

[46] Census of Business figures for 1963 cannot be used because they make no distinction between part-time and full-time employees by size of establishment.

TABLE II-9

Receipts and Employment in Beauty Shops by Store Size, 1939–58

Size of Store by Employment	Receipts per Worker			Real Receipts per Worker			Per Cent Distribution of Employment		
	1939	1948	1958	$\frac{1958}{1939}$	$\frac{1948}{1939}$	$\frac{1958}{1948}$	1939	1948	1958
0	100.00	100.00	100.00	163.64	114.67	142.70	22.17	26.23	29.30
1	114.11	114.40	103.11	147.85	114.96	128.61	23.95	20.09	12.42
2	132.79	123.93	109.89	135.41	107.01	126.53	15.96	15.85	12.47
3	147.80	135.07	121.74	134.79	104.79	128.63	10.44	9.76	8.71
4–5	159.45	146.25	129.26	132.63	105.18	126.11	10.59	10.27	10.76
6–7	164.36	155.69	136.29	135.66	108.62	124.90	5.47	4.81	6.37
8–19	181.43	178.55	142.26	128.31	112.85	113.70	8.09	8.09	13.15
20+	215.62	218.63	153.72	116.66	116.27	100.33	3.31	4.89	6.81

Source: *Census of Business*, 1939, Vol. III, Table 4A, p. 88; 1948, Vol. VI, Table 3A, p. 306; 1958, Vol. V, Table 3B, pp. 3–28.

TABLE II-10

Receipts and Payroll in Beauty Shops by Store Size, 1958

Size of Store by Employment	Receipts per Worker[a]	Average Annual Earnings per Worker[b]	Receipts / Payroll
0	3,629	2,483	1.46[c]
1	3,742	2,341	1.60
2	3,988	2,425	1.64
3	4,418	2,589	1.71
4−5	4,691	2,726	1.72
6−7	4,946	2,844	1.74
8−19	5,163	2,987	1.73
20+	5,579	3,091	1.80

[a]Full-time equivalent employees plus proprietors.

[b]The Census of Business does not report proprietors' earnings. In order to estimate them, average hourly earnings of those working 35 or more hours per week for 50−52 weeks among the self-employed as distinct from the wage and salary workers, were obtained from the 1/1,000 sample data. The ratio of the former to the latter was multiplied by the Census of Business figure for a full-time employee's wage in each store size, thus:

$$52X \; \frac{\text{Full-time weekly payroll}}{\text{Number of full-time employees}} \times \frac{\text{Average hourly earnings of self-employed}}{\text{Average hourly earnings of wage and salary workers}}$$

This estimate for proprietors in each store size was multiplied by the number of proprietors and added to the Census of Business payroll to obtain an estimate of total payroll. Total payroll was then divided by the sum of proprietors and full-time equivalent employees to obtain average annual earnings per worker.

[c]Average annual earnings of the proprietor in the 1-employee store is used to estimate proprietors' earnings in 0-employee store.

productivity in the large shops, therefore, has come from transforming idle hours into active ones.

Any increase in productivity in the largest shops of twenty or more employees occurred between 1939 and 1948. These shops are located almost exclusively in the big cities, such as New York and Chicago, where new fashions are accepted most readily. The impact of the time-saving technological innovations developed in that period was consequently felt first in these large cities. With demand already strong and continuous, processing time was decreased and the physical volume rose as customers in the big cities responded to fashion changes prompted by the new techniques, thus increasing demand.

Receipts in current dollars nearly tripled between 1939 and 1948 in the largest establishments, while in the industry as a whole receipts less than doubled over the same period. Yet the number of establishments employing twenty or more people remained almost constant over the decade and employment in them increased. The establishments with eight to nineteen employees had about equal increases in productivity in the two periods 1939–48 and 1948–58. In the earlier period they probably participated more in the benefits from new technology than from increased demand. Their receipts rose during those years about as much as did the industry as a whole, but employment fell. Smaller shops felt almost all of the impact of improved techniques and demand in the 1948–58 decade.

Except for shops with no employees, only the larger shops have increased their share of employment. The most substantial percentage increase occurred in the largest shops, which doubled their share. The eight-to-nineteen-employee establishments had the next largest increase, followed in magnitude by those with six to seven employees. The pattern is similar even among small shops, except for the very smallest. The largest percentage loss of employment occurred in the shops employing only one or two people; there was less of a loss in those employing three.

Changes in the distribution of employment by store size apparently had little effect on industry-wide changes in productivity. While the shift of business to the large, highly productive shops tended to increase productivity, the parallel growth of the zero-employee shop had the opposite effect. Of the total increase from 1939 to 1958 in output per worker of about 50 per cent, only about 3 or 4 per cent can be attributed to changes in store size. About 40 per cent is attributable to increased productivity within stores of given size. Interaction accounts for the remainder.[47]

THE TWO DECADES COMPARED

The average annual rate of increase in output per worker among beauticians has been markedly different in the decades 1939–48 and 1948–58, the rate over the second decade being more than double that of the first. Yet changes in certain factors affecting productivity, such as the distribution of age in the labor force and increases in formal education, cannot be said to have contributed more in the 1948–58 period than in 1939–48 since the changes were about equal in the two periods.

Technological change and change in demand are more likely explanations. The major time-saving innovations of the 1940's, the cold

[47] Let E_{i39}, E_{i58} = per cent distribution of employment in 1939 and 1958 respectively by size of store: P_{i39}, P_{i58} = index of receipts per employee by size of store; and i = size of store 0, 1, 2 . . . 20+ employees. Then, holding productivity constant at the 1958 level,

$$\frac{\sum_{i=0}^{20+} E_{i58}P_{i58}}{\sum_{i=0}^{20+} E_{i39}P_{i58}} = 103.40$$

or, holding productivity constant at the 1939 level,

$$\frac{\sum_{i=0}^{20+} E_{i58}P_{i39}}{\sum_{i=0}^{20+} E_{i39}P_{i39}} = 103.93.$$

Whereas, holding the distribution of employment constant at the 1958 level,

$$\frac{\sum_{i=0}^{20+} E_{i58}P_{i58}}{\sum_{i=0}^{20+} E_{i58}P_{i39}} = 139.05$$

or, holding distribution of employment constant at the 1939 level,

$$\frac{\sum_{i=0}^{20+} E_{i39}P_{i58}}{\sum_{i=0}^{20+} E_{i39}P_{i58}} = 139.76.$$

wave and the "natural" hair dyes, had heavier impact on productivity in the 1950's than in the 1940's. This is because customer acceptance was not immediate, except in the largest shops in big cities. Additional technological advances, developed in the 1950's, were not radical and were quickly adopted throughout the industry. Hence technological improvements of both periods were principally felt in the latter decade. Added to this was the large increase in demand of the 1950's, which kept operators more continuously busy, thus putting them in a position to utilize the time-saving devices to the benefit of productivity.

Between 1939 and 1948, barbers had a somewhat higher rate of increase of output per full-time worker than during the period 1948–58, 1.0 per cent contrasted with .3 per cent. As with the beautician, changes in certain factors affecting productivity, such as formal education, cannot be said to have contributed more in the 1939–48 period than in 1948–58, for they were about equal in the two periods. A factor affecting productivity adversely, namely, the aging of the labor force, changed more radically during the earlier period than during the last ten years. The drop in demand for services other than the haircut was probably sharper in 1939–48 than in 1948–58. Actually, none of the factors affecting the barber's productivity adversely changed more in the second decade than during the 1939–48 period.[48] In the absence of such a change, no satisfactory explanation can be offered for the difference in behavior between the two periods.

[48] It has been suggested that the degree of unionization among barbers in the period 1948–58 might have been greater than during 1939–48, and might have caused the rapid rise in the barber prices in the latter decade. If prices rose above equilibrium and reduced demand, this would affect productivity. However, membership in the barber's union has been reported to be as follows: 1939, 47,500; 1948, 58,600; 1958, 65,800; 1962, 51,400. Leo Troy, *Trade Union Membership, 1897–1962*, Occasional Paper 92, New York, NBER, 1965, pp. A-1 and A-10. Just the opposite situation obtained. The degree of unionization in 1939 was about 22 per cent; in 1948, 30 per cent; in 1958, 36 per cent; and in 1962, 29 per cent. The price indexes of barber services for these years were, respectively, 54, 100, 162, and 183. The rate of increase in unionization was a little higher in the 1939–48 period than in 1948–58. During the years 1958–62, unionization actually declined, so that in 1962 it was about the same as in 1948. Yet barber prices rose 89 per cent. Further, attempts were made to estimate the demand curve for haircuts in cities and states. The results were inconclusive, partly because of the inadequacy of the price data. Consequently, the effect of price on demand could not accurately be estimated.

7

SPECIAL FACTORS AFFECTING PRODUCTIVITY

UNEVEN FLOW OF DEMAND

UNLIKE those industries in which the supplier has considerable control over the rate of production, barber and beauty shops are largely dependent on the pace set by the consumer. Consumers show a marked preference for the services of barbers and beauticians toward the latter part of the week and on days preceding holidays, and the flow of traffic into shops is therefore very uneven. If enough full-time employees are hired to handle the demand at peak periods, many of these workers must remain idle and unproductive during the slack days and hours of the week.

Evidence of the low average productivity of barbers is now available as a result of publication by the Bureau of the Census of material informally called the "one-in-a-thousand sample." [49] This source provides data which show that beauty parlors have managed to meet this problem much more successfully than barber shops. The 1/1,000 sample consists of punch cards or tape containing the separate records of the characteristics of a .1 per cent sample of the population of the United States as recorded in the 1960 Census. Information such as number of hours worked and earnings for the self-employed barber, as distinct from the wage and salary worker, is provided. [50] The publication thus makes possible analysis based on average annual earnings as well as average hourly earnings, information not available before.

[49] Department of Commerce, Bureau of the Census, *U.S. Census of Population and Housing, 1960, 1/1,000, 1/10,000: Two national samples of the population of the United States,* Washington [n.d.].

[50] The self-employed among barbers are more representative of the industry than are the wage and salary workers. The 1/1,000 sample showed that they received 14 per cent more per year and 8 per cent higher hourly earnings than employees.

Occupation, age, race, sex, education, earnings, and other characteristics are provided for each individual included in the 1/1,000 sample. On the basis of this information, the average hourly earnings of workers in all nonagricultural industries in 1959 were estimated for 168 different combinations of color, age, sex, and education.[51] The "expected" [52] hourly earnings of each barber and beautician were calculated from these estimates. Then, from the 1/1,000 sample, the actual hourly earnings of each barber and beautician were calculated. Industry averages were computed for both the actual and "expected" hourly earnings, and the ratio of actual to "expected" for each industry compared.

ACTUAL AND "EXPECTED" HOURLY EARNINGS

Table II-11 gives the results. Barbers have a low ratio, .67; the beautician's is relatively high, .91. The actual hourly earnings of barbers is almost the same as that of beauticians, $1.68 compared to $1.64. Such low actual hourly earnings suggest that barbers spend much unproductive time while at work. Consider what a barber would earn in an hour if he were busy the full hour. A haircut takes twenty minutes to complete. In one hour three can be given. Prices in twenty standard metropolitan cities run from about $1.25 to $2.50. If $1.50 is assumed as the average price of a haircut, in one hour a barber would take in $4.50. An employee on a straight commission would receive about 75 per cent of this, or $3.38. The earnings in the sample data include tips. Add 10 per cent of $4.50 for tips to the $3.38, and the fully productive barber should earn $3.83 per hour. But he actually earns less than half this amount, only $1.68.

It may be noted that if it is necessary for either the barber or the beautician to be idle while waiting for customers, it is reasonable that it be the barber rather than the beautician. Alternative earnings of men are higher than those of women, but barbers and hairdressers earn about the same.[53]

The low unemployment rate among barbers supports the suggestion

[51] Unpublished material compiled at the National Bureau of Economic Research, using computer programs written by Charlotte Boschan. Persons with a job but not at work were excluded in all tabulations based on the 1/1,000 sample.

[52] I.e., the average for all workers of given age, sex, color, and education.

[53] I am indebted to Yoram Barzel of the University of Washington for this observation.

TABLE II-11

Actual and "Expected" Hourly Earnings, Barbers and Beauticians, 1959

	Number in Sample	Actual Hourly Earnings	Standard Error	"Expected" Hourly Earnings	Actual "Expected"
All barbers	160	1.68	(.07)	2.51	.67
All beauticians	261	1.64	(.15)	1.80	.91
White male barbers:					
Native, native parents	95	1.71	(.09)	2.61	.652
Native, one or both parents foreign-born	28	1.93	(.16)	2.67	.725
Foreign-born	21	1.73	(.23)	2.46	.705

Source: *U.S. Census of Population and Housing: 1960, 1/1,000, 1/10,000.*

that many of the hours spent at work are idle ones. The difference between the number of barbers in the experienced civilian labor force and employed barbers, according to the *Census of Population*, 1960, is only 1 per cent.

Historically, the barber shop was the gathering place for a kind of social activity among men. It had the air of an informal club where men could relax and exchange opinions while awaiting or receiving service. This quality has not altogether disappeared, especially among barbers themselves. Some of them, rather than leave the industry, prefer spending many idle hours for each active one in the shop, accepting as compensation the opportunity for verbal intercourse, plus the status of being "employed." Such disguised unemployment obviously results in a lowered rate of productivity for the industry.

It might be thought that the foreign-born depress barbers' earnings, but the data reject such an explanation. When earnings of the foreign-born are computed separately, as in Table II-11, the ratio of their actual to "expected" earnings is higher than that of natives with native parents, and just slightly lower than natives with one or both parents foreign-born. It should be pointed out that Table II-12 is based on white male barbers. The ratio of actual to "expected" is the same for all barbers or for white male barbers working 50–52 weeks.

That the native-born with one or both parents foreign-born have both the highest actual earnings and the highest "expected" earnings can be explained by their age distribution. Only 18 per cent of such barbers are over 55 years of age, whereas 57 per cent of the foreign-born barbers and 31 per cent of the native-born with native-born parents are over 55.

The explanation of the special age distribution seems to lie in the time pattern of immigration from Italy, a prime source of labor for barbering. During the years 1901–15, Italians entered this country at a rapid rate, averaging about 250,000 a year. The rate tapered off to about half that level by 1924,[54] when the Immigration Act went into effect, and then decreased sharply.

A majority of foreign-born parents with sons who are native-born barbers probably came from these immigrants. The oldest a son could

[54] Imre Ferenczi and Walter F. Willcox (eds.), *International Migrations*, New York, National Bureau of Economic Research, 1929, I, 195.

have been in 1958, then, was 58, if his parents were among the earliest to arrive in 1901. It is the 55-year-and-over group of barbers that has the lowest average hourly earnings, only $1.58 per hour, in contrast to $1.74 for those 39 years or less, and $1.92 for barbers between 40 and 54 years of age. The heaviest concentration of native-born barbers with foreign parents is in the 40–54 age group, whose earnings are highest.

It has been suggested that the low ratio of actual over "expected" earnings could be explained in terms of barbering being a declining industry. As such, the ratio could be expected to be around 1 for young men and very low for the older group, but the 1/1,000 data do not provide strong support for such a theory. There is a slight variation with age, as Table II-12 shows, but the ratio for men of age 25–34 is only .71.

ACCURACY OF DATA

How accurate are the data on earnings and hours reported in the 1/1,000 sample? One test of their reliability is a comparison of total earnings from the 1/1,000 sample data, based on the 1960 *Census of Population,* with personal consumption expenditures for barbers,[55] based mainly on *Census of Business* figures. It was previously pointed out that the barber receives about 75 per cent of his receipts when he is paid on a straight commission basis. The beautician customarily receives a salary plus a varying commission on her receipts in excess of twice her salary; translated into a straight commission basis, her wage would be less than 75 per cent of receipts. If the ratio of total earnings from the 1/1,000 sample to OBE estimates of personal consumption expenditures on barbering and beauty services showed a figure of about 75 percent for the former and less for the latter, this result would increase confidence in the sample data.

Dividing the total earnings by the number of workers, as reported in the sample, reveals average annual earnings of $3,916 per barber and $2,708 per beautician. In 1959 there were 172,765 barbers and 288,747 beauticians working in barber and beauty shops, according to the *Census of Population.* In addition, there were other workers employed in these establishments, 16,616 in barber shops and 23,403 in beauty

---

[55] Office of Business Economics, *Survey of Current Business,* July 1963.

TABLE II-12

Actual and "Expected" Earnings of White Male Barbers by Age, 1959

Age Group	Number in Sample	Actual Hourly Earnings	Standard Error	"Expected" Hourly Earnings	Actual "Expected"
25–34	32	1.72	(.14)	2.41	.71
35–44	21	2.03	(.18)	2.75	.74
45–54	33	1.80	(.14)	2.73	.66
Total	86	1.83	(.09)	2.61	.70

Source: *U.S. Census of Population and Housing: 1960, 1/1,000, 1/10,000.*

salons.[56] These workers must be included because the *Census of Business*, on which personal consumption expenditures depend, includes them. If earnings of $2,500 a year are assumed for these unskilled other workers, total earnings in barber shops were $717,569,000 and $824,265,000 in beauty shops. Personal-consumption expenditures in barber shops amounted to $932 million and $1,236 million in beauty shops.[57] The respective ratios of total earnings in the 1/1,000 sample to personal-consumption expenditures expressed in percentages were 77 per cent and 67 per cent. These results are sufficiently close to the figures previously cited to provide evidence supporting the accuracy of the sample data.

Another check on earnings data can be had by comparing *Census of Business* payroll figures per employee in barber and beauty shops with the average earnings per salaried barber or beautician in the 1/1,000 sample. If total payroll for barber shops is divided by all employees, the average salary is $2,867 per employee.[58] Eliminating self-employed barbers from the 1/1,000 sample results in $3,544 as the average median earnings per salaried barber. The difference between the two figures narrows when correction is made for the fact that low-salaried employees' wages are included in the *Census of Business* figures, pulling the average wage down. Approximately 10 per cent of barber-shop employees are bootblacks, porters, and other miscellaneous workers. Their average annual earnings are considerably less than those of barbers; a reduction of 5 per cent from barbers' earnings is probably approximately correct. Also, tips are included in the *Census of Population* figures, but not in the *Census of Business*. If 8 per cent is assumed

[56] These figures were estimated in the following way. There were 215,709 males working in barber and beauty shops. From them, 31,144 male hairdressers were subtracted and 4,816 female barbers added, giving 189,381 workers in barber shops. When the 172,765 barbers are subtracted, this leaves 16,616 miscellaneous workers in barber shops, assuming that all miscellaneous males worked in barber shops and all females in beauty salons. The same process was used for beauticians.

[57] *Survey of Current Business,* July 1963, p. 20. A combined figure of $2,196 million is given for barber and beauty shops and baths. The last year for which separate figures are given for all three services was 1950. At that time, baths were 1.3 per cent of the total; 1.3 per cent of $2,196 million was therefore subtracted. The remaining figure was allocated between barber and beauty shops in the same proportion as they exist in the 1958 *Census of Business* receipts, i.e., 43 per cent of total receipts by barber shops and the remainder by beauty salons. See *Census of Business,* V, 1–6.

[58] *Ibid.,* total payroll for the year divided by total paid employees for the workweek ended nearest November 15, 1958.

for tips, this reduces the average income by $269 a year, to $3,098, or $241 above the *Census of Business* figure. There is no reason, therefore, to suspect underreporting of income in the 1/1,000 sample relative to other sources.

The beautician's earnings from the 1/1,000 sample is close to the *Census of Business* figure, $2,454 contrasted with $2,437. Correction for lower wages among the miscellaneous workers need not be made for hairdressers as was necessary for barbers. A little over 50 per cent of these workers earn more than the operator, so that the average wage is not greatly affected by including them. Allowance for tips at 8 per cent brings the 1/1,000 sample figure down to $2,258, or $179 per year less than the *Census of Business* figure.

The number of hours worked is the other variable whose accuracy must be examined. One possible explanation of the low average ratio of actual to "expected" earnings for barbers is that the self-employed exaggerate their hours of work when they report them, in contrast to the wage and salary worker, who is more aware of the hours he has put in. If the self-employed are distinguished from the wage and salary worker (as has been done in Table II-13), they are seen to have higher actual hourly and "expected" earnings, and the ratio of actual to "expected" is also higher. Furthermore, average weekly hours reported by the self-employed working 35 hours or more are 50.0; wage and salary workers report 48.1. This is consistent with the figures quoted in the *Occupational Outlook Handbook* for 1957, which reports barbers as working 45 to 50 hours per week. Beauticians working 35 hours or more average 44.6 hours per week in the 1/1,000 sample data. The *Occupational Outlook Handbook* for 1961 reports full-time beauticians as working 40–44 hours per week (see also Table II-5). Comparison of earnings and figures of the 1/1,000 sample with other sources results in differences small enough to warrant confidence in the sample data.

PART-TIME WORKERS

The number of idle hours barbers spend because of the uneven flow of customer traffic has been discussed previously. Demand for beauticians' services is also highly peaked; but to ameliorate this threat to productivity, a high percentage of part-time workers are employed who work mainly during those periods when traffic is brisk.

TABLE II-13

Comparison of Hourly Earnings, White Male Self-Employed and Wage and Salary Barbers, 1959

	Number in Sample	Actual Hourly Earnings	Standard Error	"Expected" Hourly Earnings	Actual "Expected"
Self-employed	84	1.85	(.03)	2.63	.700
Wage and salary	60	1.61	(.10)	2.55	.632

Source: *U. S. Census of Population and Housing: 1960, 1/1,000, 1/10,000.*

Table II-14 shows a tripling of the percentage of part-time beauticians between 1939 and 1958, from 11.1 to 33.3 per cent; in the same period, the barbers' percentage went from 5.1 to only 10.1 per cent. In absolute numbers the contrast is more pronounced since the beauticians' percentage increase was made on an expanding base, whereas the barbers' was contracting. The use made of part-time help in the beauty salon is probably a major factor in explaining the enhanced productivity of the beautician and the barbers' failure to utilize such workers contributes to the industry's low increase in productivity.

Part-time help is often believed to be of lower quality and consequently less efficient. It might therefore be argued that increased productivity gained from fewer idle workers during slack periods might be offset by the lower productivity of the less efficient participation of part-timers. To test the validity of this objection, the 1/1,000 sample data were again utilized by computing the expected earnings for both part- and full-time beauticians separately. At the same time, the actual hourly earnings for both part-time and full-time workers were computed. The results are shown in Table II-15.

The "expected" earnings of part-timers are just about the same as for full-timers. This is true if part-time is defined as those working under 35 hours or those working fewer than 50 weeks, or both. This indicates that the quality, defined in terms of age and education, of the white female part-time beautician is equal to that of the full-time operator.

Actual hourly earnings are the same for part-timers as for full-timers who work less than 50 weeks. Of those working 50–52 weeks, the part-timer earns considerably more, $2.08 in contrast to $1.30.[59] This excess differential may be partly spurious, but the evidence suggests that a true differential does exist. The explanation probably is that the part-timers have fewer idle hours than do those working full-time.

Other evidence supports belief in the high quality of the part-timer in relation to the full-time operator. Indeed, the opinion was expressed that part-time workers in the industry are often better workers than full-timers.[60] Why this is so is related to the answer to a question which

[59] The standard errors are so large in some instances that it cannot be concluded that part-timers earn hourly more than full-timers. Tests of the differences of means at the .05 level indicate that the hypothesis that the average hourly earnings are the same for part- and full-time beauticians cannot be rejected.

[60] Interview with L. A. Freiberg.

TABLE II-14

Percentage of Part-Time Workers Among Barbers and Beauticians, 1939–58

	1939 % Part-Time	1948 % Part-Time	1958[a] % Part-Time
Barbers[b]			
Wage and salary workers	5.1	7.7	n.a.
Employed persons	n.a.	6.5	10.3
Beauticians[b]			
Wage and salary workers	11.1	20.2	n.a.
Employed persons	n.a.	23.4	33.0

Source: *Census of Population*, 1940, pp. 171–172; 1950, pp. 1B–139, 145, 151, 157; 1960, pp. 191, 201.
[a]Only male barbers and female beauticians were used so as to keep data consistent with 1939 and 1948.
[b]Those working less than 35 hours per week.

TABLE II-15

Actual and "Expected" Earnings of White Female Beauticians, Number of Hours and Weeks Worked, 1959

	Number in Sample	Actual	Standard Error	"Expected"	Actual / "Expected"
Less than 50 weeks					
Under 35 hours	40	1.85	(.57)	1.64	1.124
35 and over	61	1.86	(.55)	1.63	1.144
50–52 weeks					
Under 35 hours	21	2.08	(.62)	1.69	1.230
35 and over	84	1.30	(.08)	1.69	.771
All weeks					
Under 35 hours	61	1.95	(.41)	1.66	1.173
35 and over	145	1.49	(.21)	1.67	.891
All hours					
Under 50 weeks	101	1.86	(.41)	1.63	1.140
50–52 weeks	105	1.39	(.12)	1.69	.820
Total	206	1.56	(.19)	1.67	.934

Source: U.S. Census of Population and Housing: 1960, 1/1,000, 1/10,000.

immediately arises: If increased use of part-time help in beauty shops contributes so heavily to increased productivity, why does the barber not pursue the same policy? The answer seems to be that part-time help among males is not readily available, whereas the beautician can draw on married women whose economic situation is more conducive to acceptance of part-time work. Also, although the barber's skill is not very demanding, it is sharply different from any other male occupation. Part-time work in the field cannot, therefore, be used as a second job. According to the *Census of Population,* in 1930 only 40 per cent of female hairdressers were married, whereas today, 84 per cent of all female beauticians are married women.

In the interview previously referred to, the explanation offered for the superior performance of part-time operators was the maturity they had gained through marriage, child-bearing, and the responsibilities of managing households. The resultant sense of organization can be utilized to advantage in the beauty salon, not only by the entrepreneur but also by the employee. She often has several customers for whom she is performing different services over a given period of time. One customer may be under a dryer waiting to have her hair combed out; another has had permanent-wave lotion applied, which must be neutralized at the end of two minutes; at the same time this same operator may be shampooing a third customer who cannot be left with soap in her hair while another function is performed. It is evident how valuable a developed sense of organization is to the beautician.

Disguised unemployment may also exist among beauticians, but it takes a different form than in barber shops and has opposite repercussions on productivity. Among beauticians there are probably some who would prefer to work full-time, but who are forced to settle for part-time employment.

There is one last statistic to support the importance of the use of part-time help to explain productivity increases. Almost all white male beauticians are full-time workers, in contrast to the many part-time white female beauticians. The lower productivity of the white male beauticians in the non-South, in contrast to the white female beauticians in the same area, is reflected in a comparison of their actual over expected average hourly earnings. For male beauticians this ratio is .74 (Table II-16). For female beauticians it is substantially higher, 1.04.

TABLE II-16

Comparison of White Male Barbers and White Male and Female Beauticians, Non-South 1959

	Number in Sample	Actual Hourly Earnings	Standard Error	"Expected" Hourly Earnings	Actual "Expected"
Barbers	104	1.91	(.09)	2.62	.73
Male Beauticians	22	2.10	(.22)	2.85	.74
Female Beauticians	155	1.73	(.26)	1.67	1.04

Source: *U.S. Census of Population and Housing: 1960, 1/1,000, 1/10,000.*

EFFECTIVENESS OF RESTRICTIONS

Earlier some descriptive background of union and legislative controls was presented with the suggestion that further comments be postponed until the factors affecting productivity had been discussed. It had been anticipated, prior to use of the 1/1,000 sample to compute the barber's ratio of actual to "expected" hourly earnings, that the ratio would be greater than one, owing to the high degree of control over the industry. Actually, the ratio is considerably lower, about .7, which does not suggest that controls are very effective with respect to earnings.

Another comparison pointing to the same conclusion is that of the earnings of white male barbers and white male beauticians in the non-South.[61] The ratio of actual to expected hourly earnings is almost the same for both groups.

Evidence suggests that the attempted strong control of the barber industry has been less effective in limiting the supply of barbers than was previously believed. Illinois was earlier singled out for analysis of its barbering service.[62] The barbers' union is powerful in Chicago, which employs over 50 per cent of all barbers in Illinois, and violence has been resorted to in order to force compliance with union regulations. At the same time, legislative barriers to entry are stringent. Excluding Alaska, Illinois requires the highest number of hours of attendance at barber school, 1,872; higher than average formal education, ten years; and a very long apprenticeship, twenty-seven months. New Jersey, on the other hand, has the weakest restrictions—no length of time at barber school, no minimum education, and only the typical period of apprenticeship, eighteen months.[63]

Degree of unionization in New Jersey is presumably less than in Illinois,[64] although data on this are sketchy. However, governmental and academic sources agree that barbers in Chicago are very highly union-

---

[61] Comparison is limited to the non-South because the number of male beauticians in the South is too small to provide an adequate sample, and it is desirable to avoid the regional effect.

[62] Rottenberg, in *Aspects of Labor Economics.*

[63] *Research Report No. 33, State Barber Laws.*

[64] According to the 1960 *Census of Population,* there are 6,009 barbers in New Jersey. In unpublished material at the National Bureau of Economic Research compiled by Leo Troy, union barbers in New Jersey are estimated at 2,100 with about one-third unionized.

ized. Yet, according to the *Census of Population,* with control apparently rigid in Illinois and weak in New Jersey, the number of barbers per 1,000 males is almost identical in both states, 2.02 in the former and 2.01 in the latter. It may be thought that the importance of restrictions falls on age rather than numbers, but the median age of barbers in Illinois is 49.7 years and 50.0 in New Jersey.

As a result of the exodus to the suburbs in the postwar period, many New Jersey men continue to work in New York City. Since many of them may be presumed to use New York barbers, it may be argued that the ratio of barbers per 1,000 males in New Jersey is understated. New York City would then be expected to reap the benefit of this additional business and reflect a smaller decrease in the number of barbers per 1,000 males over the 1948–58 decade. However, it actually showed the second largest drop in the number of barbers per 1,000 males among large cities. Although this is not conclusive evidence, it certainly does not tend to support the objection.

8

CONCLUSION

SUMMARY

INCREASES in productivity, as measured by changes in constant-dollar sales per full-time equivalent worker have differed widely in two quite similar service industries. The barber's average annual rate of increase between 1939 and 1963 was .6 per cent per annum as contrasted with 1.5 for the beautician. Changes in the period 1948–63 have mainly been responsible for this difference. During these years the barber's rate of increase was only .3, whereas the beautician averaged 1.8 per cent per annum. In this period, prices in barber shops rose almost three times faster than in beauty shops. This striking contrast suggests that much may be learned about productivity by contrasting barber and beauty shops with each other.

Trends in receipts and employment in the two industries also differ sharply. Over the period 1929–63, current-dollar receipts of barber shops tripled, from $332 million to $907 million; in contrast, beauty shops have had more than a tenfold increase, from $159 million to $1,618 million. As the number of barbers has declined, the beauticians have almost trebled in number.

Among the factors traditionally believed to bear on changes in productivity, increases in capital per worker and economies of scale are of little importance in these two industries. Changes in the quality of the labor force, however, differ in the two industries and offer a partial explanation for differences in productivity. The labor force of barbers is a rapidly aging one in an industry which not only realizes no rewards from advanced age but suffers a reduction in productivity because of failing physical strength among older barbers. Cosmetology, on the other hand, offers the opportunity for improved performance as the operator matures. This improvement is evidenced both in better techniques and in a more developed sense of organization. The distribution of age of beauticians has so altered over the years as to increase productivity. Additional vocational education has probably contributed also to the productivity of beauticians; increased formal education may have helped the barber. On balance, the effect of the changing quality of the labor force appears to have been of benefit to beauty shops but not to barber shops.

The impact of the most important technological change in barbering (the safety razor) has been to reduce the demand for the barber's services in terms of fewer services per person, which has resulted in lowering productivity in the most literal sense as it has created more idle hours for the barber. Technological innovations have saved the beauty operator time, augmented the over-all demand for her services, and increased the quantity of service requested at one time. The three effects have combined to increase productivity substantially.

Among less conventional factors, one of important consequence for beauticians is the high and increasing percentage of part-time employees. These workers are largely married women with qualifications equal to the full-time operators. Concentrated use of them is made during peak demand periods; as a consequence, fewer workers sit around idly when traffic is slow. Part-timers' average hourly earnings are substantially higher than full-timers'. Barber shops use few part-time workers, and have increased their use slowly in comparison to the beautician, thus contributing to their low increase in productivity.

Barbers have had a long history of increasing control over the industry by unions, licensing laws, and trade associations. New data (the 1/1,000 sample) provide evidence that despite these efforts at control, average hourly earnings of barbers are one-third less than those of other nonagricultural workers of similar color, age, sex, and education.

IMPLICATIONS FOR FURTHER RESEARCH

The need for analysis of the individual service industries separately is evident. If two such similar industries as barber and beauty shops reflect such dissimilar productivity patterns, it is not unlikely that wide variations exist among services less closely related. This suggests that research pertaining to the service sector taken as a whole has much to gain from the more detailed findings which will result from an examination of the various parts.

The unmeasured changes in productivity of the household are apt to have more bearing on the service than on the goods sector. Wherever the skill required to perform the service is relatively low and time can be saved by the consumer if he does the work himself, he is tempted to make this transfer. Improved technology often lends impetus. Not only do the more efficient use of time and improved technology motivate the consumer; as unskilled wages rise in relation to other wages, people tend to substitute their own labor for that of the unskilled worker's.

The personal services are probably the focal point of this change in activity. Laundries present an obvious example. Electric washers and dryers are used extensively by the consumer, either at home or in large do-it-yourself centers. But the impact of the transfer of service to the home from industry is probably not limited to the more menial services. As the level of education has risen, services at one time thought difficult and therefore relegated to professionals are now attempted at home.

Analysis of only the conventional factors affecting productivity may be inadequate. The use of part-time help by barbers and beauticians may be one of the most important explanations of differences in productivity between the two industries. Many of the services, along with those of barbers and beauticians, must depend on the pace set by the consumer from day to day and hour to hour. How successfully an industry copes with this irregular flow of demand can make a vast difference in productivity. Some use self-service devices; others use part-time help; still others attempt to influence the flow of demand by lowering prices during slow parts of the week. Whatever device is used, its influence on productivity should be investigated. Immediate dependence on the pace of consumer demand is only one area. The point to be emphasized is that each service industry may be so individualistic that it is desirable that research go beyond traditional analysis of conventional primary source data to seek the kind of detailed knowledge of the industry not reflected in aggregate data.

It should be noted that several questions could not be investigated in the present study because no quantitative data existed. In other areas conclusions had to be tentatively drawn because data were meager and inadequate. It was gratifying that Arthur M. Ross, when he was sworn in as the new Commissioner of the Bureau of Labor Statistics, remarked on the need for improved statistics in the service sector:

> Much has been done to report on the newer occupations and industries, but even more remains to be done. If we need earnings and hours data for workers in manufacturing, mining, and construction, we need them just as much for those in offices, hospitals, and engineering firms. If labor turnover in the older industries is worth recording, it is even more significant in the newer industries where young people congregate. If we need to study wages, why not salaries and commissions? If we study labor-management relations in the manual trades, why not equally in the white-collar, professional, and governmental fields, including the activities of employee associations, which are not even called unions in American parlance? [65]

Data on the barber and beauty industries are lacking in these respects:

In view of the importance of the role of part-time help, their hourly earnings need to be reported and distinguished from full-time hourly earnings. Because the self-employed represent such a large portion of those employed in both barber and beauty shops, their hourly earnings should also be reported separately.

In 1939, tips were estimated by the Office of Business Economics at 5 per cent and 8 per cent for the remaining benchmark years. The question arises whether today 8 per cent is not too low an estimate. Commissions also should be given consideration, since the status of workers operating on a straight commission basis approximates that of the self-employed.

At present, no record is kept of the cost of materials used in either industry. While figures on combined shipments of equipment to both industries are available, the separate shipments to each industry are not. This is one aspect of a broader problem. Often a statistic fails to distinguish between the barber and the beauty shop, but represents the sum of the two. They should be reported on separately since their behavior is frequently dissimilar.

The current price index for beauty services is based on samples of

[65] *Monthly Labor Review*, November 1965, p. II.

prices of shampoos, sets, and permanent waves. If tinting has become as popular as is claimed, the price of this service should be included in the index. In connection with the price index, it would be helpful to make available more detailed information about the sampling process and the weights used for each of the different services in computing the average.

What direction might be taken by further research on the barber and beauty shop industries in particular? The present study has suggested that productivity is related to the flow and breadth of demand. Highly peaked demand periods interspersed among exceedingly slow periods depress productivity. Many beauty shop owners have sought to alter the flow of traffic by lowering prices during the early part of the week when demand is low. Further research might determine whether this action has been successful; if so, the feasibility of adapting it to barber shops might be investigated.

Demand can also be influenced through broadening it to include more services. The increase in the number of services offered by beauty shops stands in sharp contrast to the reduction in services offered by the barber. Beauticians believe advertising has contributed to the development of a wider variety of services demanded by the consumer. They have done little direct advertising themselves, but have reaped the rewards which have flowed from the advertisements of home products such as tints, permanents, creams, and lotions. At one time beauty parlors feared that the development and sale of these home products might hurt their business. The consensus currently, however, is that it has made females more conscious of changing styles in cosmetology, thus increasing demand and the variety of demand for beauty services.

If it is true that this effect has outweighed the adverse effect of sales to the home, consider the possibility of applying the technique to help strengthen and broaden the demand for barber services. There is some movement of fashion change taking place in barbering. Razor haircuts with higher styling are gaining acceptance. More men are becoming conscious of gray hair and are resorting to tints. So far, however, advertising is confined largely to shaving cream, after-shave lotion, razors, and razor blades. Advertisements geared to make men conscious that their present haircuts are stereotyped and warrant improvement might increase demand. Hair tinting is a service which especially requires advertising to break down inhibitions.[66] That men could be appealed to in this way is not far-fetched if it is recalled that there have been periods in history when men were far more imaginative in their tailoring and hair styling than they are now.

Another factor affecting productivity is the use of part-time help at peaked periods of demand. This is another area of sharp contrast between the two industries. There are few part-time barbers. A further study might determine whether this is primarily the result of the long periods of schooling and apprenticeship presently required of barbers. As heads of households most men require full-time employment, and some handle both a full-time and a part-time position. It is not difficult to imagine that a man would be discouraged from becoming a part-time barber, given the present laws regulating entry into barbering. If this is so, and the entry laws remain as they are, the possibility of women entering the industry to provide the necessary labor force should be considered.

It is evident from earlier remarks that productivity gains in barber shops have been limited by disguised unemployment. The industry employs a large percentage of older men who are willing to accept a work pattern of some productive activity combined with many idle hours. A problem which has received substantial attention recently concerns the destructive psychological effects on the individual created by premature retirement. As the age of retirement moves forward, the adjustment from activity to idleness has become a formidable obstacle for people to hurdle and threatens to become a sizable problem for society to solve. The barber has solved his own problem through compromise by combining some social life with some productive activity. It is difficult to imagine what society could suggest that would prove more acceptable.

This situation serves to remind us of the limitations of the concept of "measured productivity." In terms of it the barber's performance appears to be low. However, had productivity been defined in broader terms so as to include a measure of the use of productive resources, barber shops might rank high on the list. Similarly, the real estate

[66] Such advertisements for men might produce double results by increasing the service among both men and women. A recent survey of the John H. Breck Company revealed that the most frequently reported explanation given by women for not tinting their hair was husband or family disapproval.

industry offers employment to the elderly at a pace considerably slower than that of the younger agents. There may be other industries organized in this way. Future studies of productivity should investigate this aspect of the problem, and some quantitative methods need to be devised to measure and evaluate this contribution to society.

5975